Jo Pratt
madhousecookbook

Jo Pratt
madhousecookbook

DUNCAN BAIRD PUBLISHERS

LONDON

DEDICATION
To madhouse proprietors everywhere

MADHOUSE COOKBOOK
Jo Pratt

Distributed in the USA and Canada by
Sterling Publishing Co., Inc.
387 Park Avenue South
New York, NY 10016-8810

First published in the UK and USA in 2013 by
Duncan Baird Publishers, an imprint of
Watkins Publishing Limited
Sixth Floor
75 Wells Street
London W1T 3QH

A member of Osprey Group

Managing Editor: Grace Cheetham
Editor: Wendy Hobson
Art Direction and Designer: Manisha Patel
Americanizer: Beverly LeBlanc
Production: Uzma Taj
Commissioned Photography: Gareth Morgans
Food Stylist: Jo Pratt
Prop Stylist: Wei Tang

ISBN: 978-1-84899-083-8

10 9 8 7 6 5 4 3 2 1

Typeset in Myriad Pro
Color reproduction by PDQ, UK
Printed in China

For information about custom editions, special sales, premium
and corporate purchases, please contact Sterling Special Sales
Department at 800-805-5489 or specialsales@sterlingpub.com.

PUBLISHER'S NOTE
While every care has been taken in compiling the recipes for
this book, Watkins Publishing Limited, or any other persons
who have been involved in working on this publication, cannot
accept responsibility for any errors or omissions, inadvertent
or not, that mght be found in the recipes or text, nor for any
problems that might arise as a result of preparing one of these
recipes. It is important you consult a medical professional
before following any of the recipes or information contained
in this book if you have any special dietary requirements or
medical conditions. Ill or elderly people, babies, young children
and women who are pregnant or breastfeeding should avoid
recipes containing raw meat or uncooked eggs.

Notes on the recipes
Unless otherwise stated:
• Use large eggs
• Use medium fruit and vegetables
• Use fresh ingredients, including herbs and chilies
• All-purpose, self-rising and wholewheat flours should
be measured by spooning the flour into the cup measure
and then leveling the surface
• 1 tsp. = 5ml   1 tbsp. = 15ml   1 cup = 240ml

ACKNOWLEDGMENTS
A huge thanks to everyone who helped make this book…
    My children, Oliver and Rosa, and my husband Phil—the real
reasons the madhouse idea came about. The tears and tantrums
(mostly mine) have been worth it! All my family and friends for
your inspiration, ideas and taste buds.
    Everyone at Duncan Baird Publishers, in particular Grace
Cheetham, Wendy Hobson and Manisha Patel, for loving the
idea and making it great. Plus everyone in sales, marketing and
publicity for getting this book on bookshelves and in people's
homes. Gareth Morgans, Wei Tang, Poppy Campbell and Adrian
Lawrence for making everything on the photo shoots look
so fantastic and keeping it real.
    Thanks to Borra Garson and the team at DML for their
continued support in making things happen.
    Finally, a great big thanks to everyone who buys this book.
I hope it makes life less stressful in your madhouse.

PICTURE CREDIT
Wooden backgrounds pages 10–11, 76–77, 156–157:
Ingvar Bjork/Shutterstock

contents

WELCOME TO THE MADHOUSE

Oh, how my life has changed over the last few years. Gone are the days of spending a day or two preparing for elaborate dinner parties and cooking at random times when I felt like it and just because I could, with ingredients I hunted down in back-street markets and delicatessens.

That was all prechildren—now things are very different. I'm a busy mom who has to juggle work, children and all the associated chaos. I live in a madhouse! I'm always pushed for time, but I want to continue cooking food for me, my family and my friends, so it has to be simple, quick to prepare and easy to shop for—and I know I'm not alone here. Just reading around numerous websites and magazines, and chatting to other parents, it's obvious most people find cooking for their families a challenge and blinkin' hard work.

I've taken a realistic look at the situations and circumstances that cooking for the whole family entails, and it certainly isn't as straightforward as just breakfast, lunch and dinner. There are times during the week, for example, when everyone is in a rush getting to and from work/nursery/school/clubs, that can leave you feeling like a chef in a fast-food restaurant.

There are those occasions when you have no time to shop at the supermarket, so having a stack of meals in the freezer and ideas to cook from your cupboard staples, or using ingredients you grab from your local store or gas station (if you are really desperate) are a necessity.

Other situations include those rare social get-togethers where you attempt to cling onto some sort of normality and have friends over for a good old gossipy (made easy) dinner party. And, of course, some great ideas for when you get a bit of quality time

with your other half on a Saturday night and want something delicious to eat before you both fall asleep halfway through a movie you've rented.

So, to reflect my new lifestyle, I have created three main chapters—Monday-to-Friday Survival, The Busy Weekend and Cling Onto Your Social Life.

Monday-to-Friday Survival is, quite literally, recipes to help you get through the week of racing about and constantly chasing your tail. There are three sections to this chapter. Firstly, The Need for Speed, which is full of recipes that can be prepared and cooked very quickly. I'll often find I have a 10-minute window to get my kids something to eat before they start rummaging through cupboards for snacks or have a meltdown due to hunger. But it's not just the kids who need food, fast. Once they're in bed, my husband and I also need to eat before it's too late (and we have a meltdown), so there are recipes that can be converted from a kids' meal to an adult meal. The second section is Quick Prep—Leave to Cook. Here you'll find one-pot dishes that require more lengthy cooking times, so they are perfect to make before school pick-up, or to prepare while the kids are eating their supper so the meal is ready for us to eat when they're in bed. Thirdly, Speedy Sweet Treats—so much more fun and interesting than the usual fruit or yogurt options, you'll find delicious choices like Lifesaver Speedy Chocolate Pudding and Fruity Fools with a Hidden Surprise.

So, you've survived the week, but as much as you look forward to the weekend, a family house is never a quiet house. Weekends seem to be at least as busy as the weeks and we tend to complicate them by upscaling everything and often trying to fit in more than there's room for. So The Busy Weekend covers some delicious Breakfasts to give your day a great start. Then there's a section of Light Bites so you can create easy lunchtime recipes, some of which use the bare minimum for when you haven't had a chance to visit the supermarket or you've forgotten to book your online delivery, including flavorsome soups and snacks. These include imaginative meals from what you can find in the cupboard.

When you can all sit down together to share a meal, rather than eating in shifts as you tend to during the week, go to The Family Meal options for recipes you'll all enjoy.

Baking is a fun aspect to the weekend for my family, so if you are like me, you might head straight for Baking and Treats for a Sweet Tooth to find all kinds of cakes to bake together, including a couple of classic birthday cakes. Kids can get involved in many of the recipes in this chapter, which I find is good entertainment for them and a great way of getting them to be more experimental in the foods they eat.

Finally, a very important part of the weekend to me is Saturday Night—and the title says it all: Kids Are Banned. If we're not out (which is certainly less often now we have a family), my husband Phil and I will put more thought and effort into what we eat on a Saturday night, so I've selected some delicious recipes you can cook together for appetizers and nibbles to enjoy with a predinner drink, interesting main courses and a couple of desserts for a bit of delightful self-indulgence. These are all still quick and easy to prepare, but with far less urgency than on week nights.

The final chapter, Cling Onto Your Social Life, is packed with relaxed recipes for when you're doing some entertaining, many of which can be prepared ahead of time. There are some fabulous drinks and cocktails, nibbles and appetizers, impressive yet stress-free main courses and sumptuous desserts.

But, let's be practical. You're not necessarily going to make a full-on dinner party every time you invite people over, so I've made sure you can tap in and out of these sections to suit the time you have available and the energy you have left! Something as simple as having friends over for a carryout can be given a real lift if you start by offering a cocktail or homemade dips that took just a few minutes to prepare.

Time, however, is not always on your side, so look out for my Lifesavers—fabulous recipes you can retrieve from your freezer or cupboard to bring to the rescue when you are at a loss for what to serve. Dotted throughout the book, you'll find recipes like Savory Crumbs, an amazingly versatile mixture to make up and

store in the freezer, plus other recipes like my great cookie dough and freezer-to-pan salmon marinade.

Making your freezer and cupboards your friends for life is one of the best things you can do to help you keep control in your madhouse. Having them well stocked will get you out of a hole on numerous occasions. So, I've made sure there are plenty of recipes you can turn to that simply rely on a few basic ingredients from your cupboard even when you think the cupboard is bare! Plus I've added some simple How to Make recipes that are unbelievably easy and quick, but just as delicious as more complicated options.

You'll soon see this book is all about being practical with your time, physical energy and the recipes and ingredients you choose. I hate wasting food so a really important part of these recipes is offering you suggestions, tips and creative ideas on what to do with any leftovers, whether it's making a lunchbox meal for the next day, creating a whole new meal for the freezer by adding a few additional ingredients, or even making a breakfast cereal out of your weekend baking once it's past its best—all of which also make good use of your time. You'll be amazed at just what you can make out of your leftovers and pop in the freezer for another day. Fill the rest of your freezer with plenty of frozen fruit and vegetables, prepared pastry, bread, meat and fish.

My main piece of advice to avoid getting stressed out when cooking is to take a moment and read through the recipes before you start cooking them, as—if your house is anything like mine—you're bound to be distracted by someone or something while you are actually cooking. If you don't have certain ingredients, don't panic. Try to be relaxed and practical about what ingredients you do have—be creative and substitute.

So, here's to being the ultimate mom and dad, the best hosts and *über* partners. Happy juggling and enjoy!

Jo Pratt
x .

MONDAY-TO-FRIDAY SURVIVAL

Quick, simple, clever and delicious ...

Five days, 1001 things to do ... work, school, after-school clubs, homework, making sure you watch your favorite TV show, the laundry, the shopping, the cleaning, finishing that best-selling novel, making sure you've called your parents to let them know everyone is okay and, of course, cooking and eating (not necessarily in that order).

The ambition of this chapter is to make the cooking and eating part a little bit easier and more enjoyable. The recipes are simple, quick, flavorsome and clever, with tips like how to cook a dish for your children, then convert it into something the adults will enjoy later when the kids are in bed. Even the quantities have been designed with your lifestyle in mind. In The Need for Speed and Speedy Sweet Treats, most of the recipes are for two adult-size portions or four child-size portions, so you can mix and match however it suits you. Plus, of course, they are easy to adjust to make more or less. In the Quick Prep—Leave to Cook section, I've made the recipes to serve more portions as they take a little longer to cook, so you have plenty to feed the whole family or extras to freeze for almost instant meals another day.

You'll find lots of other top tips, lifesaving ideas and great ways to use leftovers, too. And, of course, every recipe has been stress-tested in my own kitchen with my family and they work ... no, they rock!

I love to make this recipe on a Friday night. It's great for using up leftover potatoes and can be made quicker than the time it takes to organize a carryout. I always keep a bag of frozen spinach in the freezer—it's really convenient for all sorts of dishes. If I have some fresh spinach in the refrigerator, however, I just roughly chop a couple big handfuls and add them to the pan when the curry is almost ready.

Chicken, Potato and Spinach Curry in a Hurry

MAKES 2 adult or 4 child portions
PREPARATION TIME 10 minutes
COOKING TIME 20 minutes

1½ tablespoons sunflower
   or vegetable oil
1 onion, thinly sliced
2 boneless, skinless chicken breast
   halves, diced
2 garlic cloves, crushed
1½-inch piece gingerroot, peeled
   and grated
1 tablespoon garam masala
½ teaspoon cayenne pepper
1 can (15-oz.) crushed tomatoes
7 ounces cooked new potatoes, halved
   if large (canned potatoes are also fine)
1 cup frozen spinach, thawed
sea salt and freshly ground black pepper

TO SERVE
naan bread
Cucumber Raita (see page 25)
   or bought raita
mango chutney (optional)

1 Heat the oil in a large pan over low heat, add the onion and cook a few minutes until soft. Increase the heat to medium, add the chicken, garlic and ginger and fry 3 to 4 minutes until the chicken turns opaque. Stir in the garam masala and cayenne and continue to cook about 1 minute.

2 Add the tomatoes, potatoes and ⅔ cup water. Bring to a boil, then reduce the heat, cover loosely with a lid and leave the curry to simmer about 10 minutes until the chicken is cooked through.

3 Stir in the spinach and season lightly with salt and pepper, then continue cooking 2 to 3 minutes longer, stirring occasionally.

4 Serve the curry on its own or with naan bread, raita and mango chutney, if you like.

Leftovers for the freezer
frozen ginger
If you have a large piece **gingerroot** left over, don't leave it lurking in the corner of your refrigerator to deteriorate gradually. Put all or some of it in a sandwich bag, seal, label and store in the freezer—it will keep for several months. When a recipe calls for grated gingerroot, it will grate really easily straight from frozen—no need to thaw or peel.

This is one of my kids' favorites, and it is a great way to use up leftover rice. You can use ham or other ingredients the kids really like instead of the chicken, if you prefer, so you can be sure they'll love it.

Very Special Fried Rice

MAKES 2 adult or 4 child portions
PREPARATION TIME 10 minutes
COOKING TIME 7 minutes

2 boneless, skinless chicken breast halves, thinly sliced
2 tablespoons soy sauce
2 tablespoons honey
1 tablespoon sunflower or vegetable oil
4 scallions, finely chopped
1 cup green beans, cut into pieces
1 carrot or zucchini, peeled and coarsely grated
1⅔ cups cooked basmati rice (either bought precooked or leftovers)
½ cup corn kernels, rinsed if canned or thawed if frozen
½ cup drained canned diced pineapple
1 egg, beaten

1 Put the chicken meat in a bowl and stir in the soy sauce and honey. Leave to one side to marinate a few minutes.

2 Heat the oil in a wok or large frying pan over medium heat, add the chopped and grated vegetables and stir-fry about 1 minute. Add the chicken and the marinade and stir-fry a few minutes, or until the chicken is cooked through. Add the rice, corn and pineapple and stir-fry about 2 minutes until the rice is hot right through.

3 Pour in the egg, stirring to mix the egg through the rice, and fry about 30 seconds.

4 Serve with chopsticks for an authentic touch (and the entertainment value in most cases).

How to cook
perfect basmati rice

Start with a good-quality basmati rice and measure out the amount you need. As a general rule, **1 part rice** to **2 parts water** is the ratio, so to make life easy, measure the quantity of rice in a cup and use the same cup to measure the water. Unless a recipe states otherwise, ⅓ **cup is usually sufficient per adult portion**. Pop the rice in a strainer and rinse under cold water about 1 minute to remove the excess starch. Shake off as much water as you can, then tip the rice into a pan. Now measure in twice as much cold water and add **a pinch of salt**. Bring to a boil over high heat. Immediately reduce the heat to low, cover with a tight-fitting lid and leave untouched 10 minutes. Turn off the heat and, with the lid still on, leave the rice to stand 5 minutes. Run a fork through the rice and you will have delicious, fluffy basmati rice.

It's great to experiment with different filling options depending on what you like and can get your hands on. Just don't fill overfill the quesadillas, or they will be too difficult to flip over. They will still taste good, but might look a bit battered! Our household favorite fillings include baked beans, grated cheddar cheese and a shake of Worcestershire sauce, or grated cheddar cheese with sliced avocado, fresh cilantro leaves and tomato salsa.

Chicken, Cheese and Corn Quesa-d-easies

MAKES 2 adult or 4 child portions
PREPARATION TIME 5 minutes
COOKING TIME 12 minutes

4 wheat or corn tortillas
1 handful arugula leaves, to serve

FOR THE CHICKEN, CHEESE AND CORN FILLING
2 large handfuls grated cheddar cheese
2 large handfuls leftover cooked chicken, torn into small pieces
4 tablespoons corn kernels, rinsed if canned or thawed if frozen
2 tablespoons sweet chili dipping sauce, plus extra for serving (optional)
1 tablespoon chopped parsley leaves

1 Heat a skillet to medium heat. Put one tortilla in the pan and sprinkle half of the filling ingredients over. Cover with the second tortilla and cook 2 to 3 minutes.

2 Gently flip the whole quesadilla over and cook 2 to 3 minutes longer until the bottom is golden and the cheese melts.

3 Remove the quesadilla from the pan and keep it warm while you cook the second one. Transfer them to a board and cut into quarters, using a pizza wheel if you have one. Serve hot with the arugula leaves and extra chili dipping sauce, if you like.

Leftovers for a pizza
tortilla pizzas

This is the quickest, easiest pizza kids (and adults) of all ages enjoy. Simply spread **1 tablespoon tomato paste** or **sun-dried tomato paste** onto a piece of **wheat tortilla**. Scatter **grated cheddar cheese** (or half cheddar and half grated mozzarella) over. Leave plain or add **chopped cooked ham**, **salami**, **shredded chicken**, **drained and flaked canned tuna**, **sliced olives**, **corn kernels**, **sliced onion** or **halved cherry tomatoes**. Don't add too much or the pizza will be top heavy. Put the tortilla on a cookie sheet and cook in an oven heated to 425°F 8 to 10 minutes until the cheese melts.

P.S. It is worth making one more than you think you'll need of these, because they will be gone in seconds!

Here's one for all you lovers of yeast extract out there. Serve this with your favorite vegetables, or, to make it a bit more grown up, in a chunk of ciabatta with arugula, guacamole (see below), sliced tomato and mayonnaise for a club sandwich with a difference.

Crunchy Love-it-or-Hate-it Chicken

MAKES 2 adult or 4 child portions
PREPARATION TIME 15 minutes using made Savory Crumbs, or 25 minutes from scratch
COOKING TIME 5 minutes

2 boneless, skinless chicken breast halves
1 egg white
2 teaspoons yeast extract
1 cup Savory Crumbs (see page 30) or plain bread crumbs
sunflower oil, for frying

TO SERVE
baked beans or vegetables of your choice
homemade Oven-Baked French Fries (see page 148) or bought oven-baked fries, mashed potatoes or rice

1 Put the chicken breasts in between two sheets of wax paper and bash with a rolling pin to flatten slightly. Cut into ½- to ¾-inch strips.

2 Lightly beat the egg white and yeast extract together until just frothy. Add the chicken to the mixture and leave to stand a couple minutes.

3 Toss the chicken pieces, a few at a time, in the savory crumbs. (Pieces of crumb-coated chicken can be frozen up to 3 months. Thaw them thoroughly before frying.)

4 Meanwhile, pour enough oil into a skillet to cover the surface and heat over medium heat. Add the chicken pieces and fry a few minutes on each side until golden, crunchy and cooked through. Drain well on paper towels.

5 Serve with baked beans or vegetables and your favorite fries, mashed potatoes or rice.

How to make

homemade guacamole

Put the flesh of **2 ripe avocados** in the bowl of a small food processor or suitable container for a hand blender. Remove the seeds from **1 tomato** and roughly chop the flesh, then add it to the avocados with **1 garlic clove**, the **juice of ½ lime** and **a few cilantro leaves**. Whiz to a rough or smooth consistency. If you want some spice, add **1 seeded and finely chopped red chili** or **a few good splashes hot-pepper sauce**. For crunch, add **½ finely chopped red onion**. Season to taste with **sea salt** and **freshly ground black pepper** before serving. If you are not planning to serve the guacamole straightaway, push the avocado pit into the guacamole to help prevent it from turning brown. Covered with plastic wrap, it will store in the refrigerator up to a day.

We all resort to pasta recipes for quick and easy meals—so here's another to add to your repertoire. This is one of those dishes I'll cook when we're in the mood for comfort food, and the ingredients are usually sitting in my refrigerator. If I don't have any cream, sour cream or plain yogurt makes a convenient substitute.

Bacon, Leek and Brie Penne

MAKES 2 adult or 4 child portions
PREPARATION TIME 10 minutes
COOKING TIME 15 minutes

9 ounces dry penne
a drizzle olive oil
⅔ cup diced bacon lardons or pancetta
1 leek, sliced
½ cup white wine
½ cup light cream
3½ ounces Brie, cut into small chunks
a pinch dried chili flakes
sea salt and plenty of freshly ground
   black pepper

1 Bring a large pan of lightly salted water to a boil, add the penne and return to a boil. Leave to boil about 10 minutes until just tender.

2 Meanwhile, heat the oil in a large skillet over medium heat, add the bacon and fry 5 minutes, or until golden. Drain off any excess fat, then add the leek to the pan. Fry over low heat 5 minutes, or until soft. Pour in the wine and bring to a boil. Stir in the cream, Brie, chili flakes and black pepper.

3 Drain the pasta and add to the sauce. Stir gently over low heat a minute or so, then serve.

Leftover lardons
spicy bacon and tomato sauce

If you have opened a large package of lardons or pancetta, it's worth making a quick pasta sauce for the refrigerator or freezer. Fry the **lardons** in **a drizzle of olive oil** until golden. Add **a can (15-oz.) crushed tomatoes** and **a good pinch each dried chili flakes** and **dried oregano**. Simmer 10 minutes, or until thicker. Stir in **2 tablespoons mascarpone** or **cream cheese** and some **sea salt** and **freshly ground black pepper**, then keep in the refrigerator a couple days or in the freezer up to 3 months. Heat and toss with cooked pasta when needed.

We love carbonara in our house, but the traditional rich, creamy version is sometimes a bit too much for midweek. Try this lighter option if you're a fan—it even contributes to your daily vegetable total.

Spaghetti and Zucchini Carbonara

MAKES 2 adult or 4 child portions
PREPARATION TIME 15 minutes
COOKING TIME 12 minutes

9 ounce dry spaghetti
1 tablespoon olive oil
1 cup finely diced smoked bacon
1 zucchini, grated
1 garlic clove, crushed
2 eggs, lightly beaten
½ cup mascarpone
¼ cup freshly grated Parmesan cheese
sea salt and freshly ground black pepper

1 Bring a large pan of lightly salted water to a boil, add the spaghetti and return to a boil. Leave to boil about 10 minutes until it is just tender.

2 Meanwhile, heat the oil in a large skillet over medium heat, add the bacon and fry 5 to 8 minutes until golden. Add the zucchini and garlic and fry a couple of minutes to take away the initial rawness.

3 In a bowl, mix together the eggs, mascarpone and Parmesan and season lightly with salt and pepper.

4 As soon as the spaghetti is cooked, remove it from the water with a pair of tongs and put it straight into the pan with the bacon and zucchini and toss around. Finally, add the egg mixture.

5 Remove the skillet from the heat and toss together to coat the spaghetti in the sauce. The heat from the spaghetti will cook the egg just enough without scrambling it. Serve immediately.

Leftovers transformed
spaghetti fritters

Any leftover spaghetti carbonara can be transformed into really delicous fritters that are perfect for a quick, hot lunch or even cold in school lunchboxes. Simply take the leftovers and snip the **spaghetti** a couple of times with a pair of scissors into smaller pieces. Mix with enough **beaten egg** to bind. You can also add some **peas**, **corn kernels** or more **grated zucchini** here, too. Heat **a drizzle of olive oil** in a skillet. Add spoonfuls of the spaghetti mixture and fry until golden on both sides. Drain on paper towels and serve hot or cold.

This is great recipe that can be made as a family meal or, once you have prepared everything, you can halve the mixture and cook one half for the kids to enjoy for an early dinner and the other for an adult meal later. It's ideal for using up leftover potatoes, and it really doesn't matter if they break up when you chop them. In fact, they become even crunchier that way.

Corned Beef and Corn Hash with a Dash of Flexibility

MAKES 2 adult or 4 child portions
PREPARATION TIME 10 minutes
COOKING TIME 20 minutes

2 to 3 tablespoons olive oil
1 onion, thinly sliced
1¾ cups cooked potatoes cut into small chunks
12 ounces canned corned beef, crumbled into chunks
1½ cups canned corn kernels, rinsed
a shake Worcestershire sauce
a pinch dried chili flakes (optional)
2 handfuls baby spinach leaves, roughly chopped (or use thawed)
sea salt and freshly ground black pepper

TO SERVE
fried or poached eggs (optional)
sweet chili sauce or ketchup

1 Heat 1 tablespoon of the oil in a skillet, add the onion and fry over low heat about 5 minutes until soft and starting to turn golden.

2 Transfer the onion to a bowl and add the potatoes, corned beef, corn kernels, Worcestershire sauce and chili flakes, if using. Season lightly with salt and pepper. Mix to combine and either divide into individual portions or cook as one large hash. (The hash can be divided into portions before cooking and any that isn't cooked straightaway can be kept in the refrigerator for later.)

3 Heat the remaining oil in the skillet over medium-high heat, add the hash and cook about 5 minutes, stirring to heat everything through. Stir in the spinach and continue to fry about 5 minutes, stirring just until everything is hot, then leave, without stirring, about 5 minutes until the corned beef and potatoes turn golden brown and crisp on the edges.

4 Serve the hash as it is or topped with a fried or poached egg, if you like, and a sauce of your choice.

Serve this super-speedy steak sandwich and it will earn you lots of brownie points. The crucial ingredient is the pan-fried avocado—oddly, it smells and tastes like bacon! French fries are a great accompaniment— you can make your own (see page 148) or just throw in bought ready-to-bake fries, and I find the shoestring variety cooks best, because they become crunchier than the fatter ones. Oh, and use any bread you have to hand—you don't have to use expensive bread.

Speedy Steak and Pan-Fried Avocado Club Sandwich

MAKES 2 adult or 4 child portions
PREPARATION TIME 10 minutes
COOKING TIME 5 minutes

1 tablespoon Dijon mustard
1 tablespoon honey
a shake Worcestershire sauce
2 minute steaks
a drizzle olive oil
1 small avocado, pitted, peeled and sliced
6 slices bread
¼ small iceberg lettuce, shredded
2 tablespoons mayonnaise
a squeeze lemon juice
2 tomatoes, thinly sliced
sea salt and freshly ground black pepper

TO SERVE
homemade Oven-Baked French Fries (see page 148) or bought ready-to-bake French fries
homemade Perfect Coleslaw (see page 93) or bought coleslaw

1 Mix together the mustard, honey and Worcestershire sauce, then spread or brush the mixture over both sides of the steaks.

2 Heat a griddle or skillet over high heat until hot enough to start smoking. Put the steaks in the hot pan and cook about 1 minute on each side (depending on their thickness) until lightly colored. At the same time, drizzle the oil over the avocado and season lightly with salt and pepper. Fry the avocado in the same pan 1 to 2 minutes on each side until golden brown.

3 Meanwhile, lightly toast the bread on both sides.

4 Mix the lettuce with the mayonnaise and lemon juice and divide half the mixture between two pieces toast. Top each with the pan-fried avocado and then with a second piece of toast. Spread the remaining lettuce on top, then add the steak. Add the tomatoes and season lightly with salt and pepper, then finish with the last pieces of toast. Press down lightly.

5 Cut each sandwich in half or into quarters, secure with toothpicks and serve with French fries and coleslaw.

I find Monday-to-Friday survival is a little easier when I'm cooking with just one pan. There are fewer distractions and, therefore, fewer things that can go wrong. Just follow the step-by-step methods and the results will be delicious. If you don't have smoked salmon, try this with smoked mackerel or trout. You can even use pieces of leftover roast chicken, turkey or lamb, which are equally delicious. This recipe is also a good way to use up leftover rice.

One-Pan Hot-Smoked Salmon Biryani

MAKES 2 adult or 4 child portions
PREPARATION TIME 15 minutes
COOKING TIME 15 minutes

1 tablespoon sunflower oil
1 onion, thinly sliced
2 garlic cloves, crushed
¾-inch piece gingerroot, peeled and grated
1 handful golden raisins
1 tablespoon garam masala
7 ounces broccoli, tenderstem broccoli, asparagus, green beans or snow peas, chopped
1⅔ cups cooked basmati rice
5 ounces hot-smoked salmon fillets, flaked into pieces
1 handful toasted slivered almonds
a squeeze lemon juice
4 tablespoons plain yogurt, sour cream or crème fraîche
1 small handful cilantro or mint leaves or dill, chopped
sea salt and freshly ground black pepper

1 Heat the oil in a large skillet over low heat and fry the onion about 5 minutes until it becomes golden. Stir in the garlic, ginger, golden raisins and garam masala and cook 1 minute. Add the green vegetables and fry together 2 to 3 minutes longer until the vegetables are just tender.

2 Stir in the rice, salmon and almonds. Season lightly with salt and pepper. Stir-fry over medium heat a few minutes until the rice and salmon are heated through.

3 Gently stir through the lemon juice, yogurt and herbs and serve immediately.

How to make

cucumber raita

Blend together **⅔ cup Greek yogurt**, **¼ seeded cucumber**, **1 small handful chopped mint** or **cilantro leaves** and **a pinch of sea salt** until well combined. Serve straightaway or you can keep this in the refrigerator up to a day.

Pull the soybeans and peas our of the freezer and marinate the salmon while you're getting the kids' school bags ready for the next day, polishing school shoes, washing gym clothes (and hoping they dry in time) and making sure your kids have cleaned their teeth before they go to bed. Once that's all done, this is a delicious recipe for two that takes no time at all to cook.

Honey-Miso Salmon with Warm Green Salad

MAKES 2 adult or 4 child portions
PREPARATION TIME 10 minutes, plus at
   least 30 minutes marinating (optional)
COOKING TIME 5 minutes

FOR THE HONEY-MISO SALMON
2 salmon fillets, skinned
½ recipe quantity Honey-Miso Marinade
   (see below)
sunflower or olive oil, for brushing
1 teaspoon toasted sesame seeds

FOR THE WARM GREEN SALAD
7 ounces broccoli or tenderstem broccoli
⅔ cup sugar snap peas
½ cup frozen soybeans or fava beans,
   thawed
⅔ cup frozen peas, thawed
2 scallions, thinly sliced on an angle
juice of ½ lime
1 teaspoon toasted sesame oil
1 tablespoon olive oil
1 small handful cilantro leaves, chopped
sea salt and freshly ground black pepper

1 Put the salmon in a shallow, nonmetallic bowl, then pour the marinade over and rub it into the fillets. Cover the bowl and leave the salmon to marinate in the refrigerator about 30 minutes. You can leave it longer if you have the time, but it can also be cooked straightaway, if necessary.

2 Brush a skillet or griddle with a little oil over medium-high heat, add the salmon and cook a couple of minutes on each side until just cooked through.

3 Meanwhile, bring a pan of water to a boil, put the broccoli, sugar snap peas, soybeans and peas in a steamer basket and steam up to 5 minutes until tender.

4 Transfer broccoli and sugar snap peas to a bowl and toss with the remaining salad ingredients, seasoning lightly with salt and pepper.

5 Scatter the sesame seeds over the hot salmon and serve with the warm salad.

Lifesaver marinade
honey-miso marinade
Make up a batch of this marinade and store it in a jar in the refrigerator up to 2 weeks. Use it to flavor fish, chicken, pork or beef before frying or broiling. These measurements will give you 4 adult portions, but you can increase the quantities as much as you like. Mix together: **2 tablespoons honey, 2 tablespoons white miso paste, 2 teaspoons rice vinegar** or **lime juice, 2 tablespoons light soy sauce** and **1½-inch piece gingerroot**, peeled and finely grated.

I've tried to write the recipes in this section using ingredients most of us have in our cupboards or refrigerators. There might be a few things you will need to pick up at the supermarket, but nothing out of the ordinary. This recipe, for example, combines leftover cooked potatoes with canned tuna, frozen peas, olive oil, scallions and lemons—all fairly standard staples. All you need to remember to add to your shopping list is parsley (buy a growing pot) and semolina or polenta, both of which last ages, then these little beauties can be made as a delicious, quick midweek meal. Instead of tuna, try canned salmon or even leftover cooked salmon, cod or other white fish. Peas can be swapped for the corn kernels, or try mixed frozen vegetables, and other herbs can be used instead of parsley.

Pea and Tuna Fish Cakes with Caper and Lemon Mayonnaise

MAKES 2 adult or 4 child portions
PREPARATION TIME 15 minutes if using
   previously cooked mashed potatoes
COOKING TIME 10 minutes

2 cups cooked potatoes, peeled,
   if necessary
6 ounces canned tuna, drained and
   flaked
4 scallions, finely chopped
½ cup frozen peas, thawed
1 tablespoon chopped parsley leaves
finely grated zest of 1 lemon
1 cup semolina or polenta (or 1¼ cups
   Savory Crumbs on page 30)
3 tablespoons olive oil
sea salt and freshly ground black pepper

**FOR THE CAPER AND LEMON
   MAYONNAISE (OPTIONAL)**
4 tablespoons mayonnaise
1 tablespoon chopped capers
1 tablespoon chopped parsley leaves
1 tablespoon lemon juice
a pinch cayenne pepper

TO SERVE
ketchup or mayonnaise (optional)
mixed green salad
corn kernels, rinsed if canned or thawed
   if frozen and cooked until hot
cucumber sliced

1 Put the potatoes in a large bowl and mash them. Add the tuna, scallions, peas, parsley and lemon zest, and season lightly with salt and pepper. Mix until well combined.

2 Using wet hands to stop the mixture sticking to you, shape into fish cakes—large or small, it's up to you. Lightly coat each one all over with the semolina and cook straightaway or chill until needed.

3 Heat the oil in large skillet over medium heat, add the fish cakes and fry 4 to 5 minutes on each side until golden brown. You might need to do this in batches, depending on the size of your skillet. Take care not to have the heat too high, because you want to make sure they heat all the way through before the outside becomes too brown.

4 If you are making the caper and lemon mayonnaise, simply mix together all the ingredients. (Any leftovers will keep in the refrigerator up to a week in a sealed screw-top jar.)

5 Serve the fish cakes with the caper and lemon mayonnaise, if you like, (or kids will probably opt for ketchup or plain mayonnaise). These are great on their own or served with a fresh salad.

This is what I call a flexi-recipe—either a family meal, or one where the kids eat earlier and the adults enjoy the meal (perhaps with a glass of wine) when the kids are in bed. Prepare and freeze the fish sticks ahead of time, then just cook when you need them.

Fish Stick Tortillas

MAKES 2 adult or 4 child portions
PREPARATION TIME 10 minutes using
  prepared Savory Crumbs or 20 minutes
  from scratch
COOKING TIME 6 minutes

FOR THE FISH FINGERS
9 ounces thick fish fillet, such
  as salmon, cod, haddock, pollack
  or other white fish, skinned
2 tablespoons all-purpose flour
1 egg, lightly beaten
¾ cup Savory Crumbs
  (see below)
2 to 3 tablespoons olive oil
a pinch sea salt (optional)

TO SERVE
wheat or corn tortillas
choose any accompaniment, including:
• shredded lettuce or arugula
• tomato salsa, hot-pepper sauce,
  ketchup
• mayonnaise (flavored with garlic, lime
  or lemon juice), sour cream
• sliced tomatoes
• sliced avocado
• Homemade Guacamole (see page 18)
  or bought guacamole

1 Cut the fish into 12 equal pieces and season lightly with salt, if you like.

2 Put the flour, egg and savory crumbs into three separate medium sandwich bags or shallow bowls. First, coat the fish sticks, a few at a time, in flour, then egg and, finally, turn gently in the crumbs so they are evenly coated. (The fish sticks can be prepared to this stage and cooked straightaway, kept in the refrigerator up to a day or frozen up to 3 months.)

3 To cook, heat a skillet over medium heat and add the oil. If you plan to cook just a few, use less oil. Once the oil is hot, add the fish sticks and cook 2 to 3 minutes on each side until golden and cooked through. Alternatively, if you have the oven on at 400°F (to cook some ready-to-bake French fries or potato wedges, see page 148, for example), lightly brush the fish sticks in the oil, put on a hot baking sheet lined with parchment paper and cook about 6 minutes until golden, turning halfway. (If cooking from frozen, add a couple of minutes on each side, and fry or bake until completely cooked through.)

4 Once the fish sticks are cooked, either warm your tortillas in a microwave or lightly toast under the broiler, then tailor-make your tortillas to everyone's liking. Serve hot.

Lifesaver for the freezer

savory crumbs

Simply whiz **7 ounces white bread** (with or without the crust) to make fine crumbs in a food processor. Add **⅓ cup fine cornmeal, polenta** or **semolina** and **⅔ cup finely grated fresh Parmesan cheese** and put into one large or a few smaller freezer bags. You can also shake in other flavorings before you freeze or add just before using, such as **grated lemon**, **lime** or **orange zest**, **chopped herbs**, **finely chopped nuts**, **dried herbs**, **garam masala**, **paprika**, **chili powder**, **Chinese five-spice**, or **jerk** or **Cajun seasoning**. Put the crumbs in the freezer, then, when just frozen, shake the bag to break up the crumbs so they don't freeze in a solid clump.

When the kids are STARRRRVING and you need something quick, these sauces are lifesavers. There's no need to be too specific about quantities. They are guidelines to help you to please grumbling tummies.

Very, Very, Very Quick Pasta Dishes

EACH SAUCE MAKES 2 adult or 4 child portions
PREPARATION TIME 5 minutes
COOKING TIME 10 minutes

SMOKED SALMON, CREAM CHEESE AND CHIVE FARFALLE

2¾ cups dry farfalle
1 cup plus 2 tablespoons cream cheese
5 tablespoons milk
4 ripe tomatoes, seeded and diced
6 ounces smoked salmon, cut into small
   pieces
1 handful chives, finely snipped

1 Bring a pan of water to a boil, add the pasta and return to a boil. Boil about 10 minutes until just tender. Drain well, then return the pasta to the hot pan.

2 Meanwhile, put the cream cheese and milk into a small pan and heat gently, stirring until the cream cheese melts. Add the tomatoes and stir about 1 minute, then stir in the smoked salmon and chives. Pour the sauce over the drained pasta and stir together. Serve hot.

SAUSAGE, PESTO AND TOMATO PENNE

a drizzle olive oil
4 link pork sausages, skinned and
   broken into chunks
1 can (15-oz.) crushed tomatoes
2 tablespoons pesto sauce
4 tablespoons cream cheese (optional)
2¾ cups dry penne

1 Heat the oil in a small pan over medium heat, add the sausage chunks and fry 5 minutes, or until cooked and lightly colored, breaking down the meat with a wooden spoon. Stir in the tomatoes and bring to a simmer, then cook 5 minutes. Stir in the pesto. Stir in the cream cheese, if you like, for a creamier sauce.

2 Meanwhile, bring a pan of water to a boil, add the pasta and return to a boil. Boil about 10 minutes until just tender. Drain well, then return to the hot pan. Pour the sauce over the drained pasta and stir together. Serve hot.

CREAMY PEA, BASIL AND HAM LINGUINE

9 ounces dry linguine
1 cup plus 2 tablespoons mascarpone
  or cream cheese
2 tablespoons milk
3 tablespoons tomato or sun-dried
  tomato paste
1 large handful frozen peas
1 small handful basil leaves, chopped
4 slices cooked ham, finely chopped
sea salt and freshly ground black pepper

1 Bring a pan of water to a boil, add the pasta and return to a boil. Boil about 10 minutes until just tender. Drain well, then return the pasta to the hot pan.

2 Meanwhile, put the mascarpone, milk and tomato paste in a saucepan over low heat and stir until the cheese melts. Add the peas, basil and ham and stir 2 minutes until heated through. Season lightly with salt and pepper. Pour the sauce over the drained pasta and stir together. Serve hot.

BUTTERY MUSHROOM AND PARMESAN FUSILLI

2¾ cups dry fusilli
3 tablespoons butter
3 cups sliced button or cremini
  mushrooms
2 garlic cloves, crushed
juice of 1 small lemon
2 tablespoons chopped basil or parsley
  leaves (optional)
⅔ cup freshly grated Parmesan cheese
a splash heavy cream (optional)

1 Bring a pan of water to a boil, add the pasta and return to a boil. Boil about 10 minutes until just tender. Drain well, then return the pasta to the hot pan.

2 Meanwhile, melt the butter in a skillet over medium heat and add the mushrooms. Cook a few minutes until they are soft and starting to color. Add the garlic and lemon juice, and the basil, if using, and cook 2 minutes longer. Spoon the sauce over the drained pasta, sprinkle with the Parmesan and stir together. For an extra-creamy finish, you can add a splash of heavy cream, if you like. Serve hot.

Always, always have these ingredients in your pantry or cupboards and you will never be without a delicious evening meal. Apart from the onion, everything comes in a package, jar or can and lasts for ages. If you don't have anchovies, adding a can of drained and flaked tuna makes an ideal substitute.

Pantry Pasta Puttanesca

MAKES 2 adult or 4 child portions
PREPARATION TIME 15 minutes
COOKING TIME 15 minutes

2 tablespoons olive oil
1 onion, finely diced
½ red chili, seeded (or seeds left in for a spicier finish) and thinly sliced or ¼ teaspoon dried chili flakes
4 bottled or canned anchovy fillets, drained and finely chopped
1 can (15-oz.) crushed tomatoes
½ teaspoon dried oregano
1½ cups ripe kalamata olives, halved and pitted
1 tablespoon capers, rinsed and chopped if large
2¾ cups dry pasta, such as penne
freshly grated Parmesan cheese, for sprinkling
sea salt and freshly ground black pepper

1 Heat the oil in a large skillet over medium heat, add the onion and chili and fry about 5 minutes until the onion is soft but not colored. Add the anchovies and cook a few minutes longer, stirring all the time. Stir in the tomatoes, oregano, olives and capers. Bring to a boil and season lightly with salt and pepper, then reduce the heat to low and leave to simmer 8 to 10 minutes.

2 Meanwhile, bring a pan of lightly salted water to a boil, add the pasta and return to a boil. Boil about 10 minutes until just tender. Drain well.

3 Add the pasta to the sauce and stir well. Serve sprinkled with plenty of Parmesan cheese.

Lifesaver for handy dinners
storing the puttanesca sauce in jars
If you have the ingredients, it's a real lifesaver if you make double (or more) of the sauce and store it in jars to use when needed. All you need to do is divide the cooked sauce into hot, sterilized jars and seal loosely with a lid. Put them in a roasting pan lined with a folded dish towel and fill ¾ inch deep with hot water. Put in a heated oven at 315°F 25 minutes, then carefully remove from the pan and seal tightly. Store in a cool, dark place and use within 6 months. Once open, store in the refrigerator and use within a few days.

A really simple recipe that you can call Asian Shrimp and Noodle Broth if you want to give it a more upscale name. This is a perfect dish to make for kids as well as adults. It's almost as easy as heating a bought one-pot meal. Just make sure you are careful which chili you use, if you are going to serve it to your kids, because they vary so much in their degree of heat. As a general rule, the longer they are, the milder they are.

One-Pot Noodles

MAKES 2 adult or 4 child portions
PREPARATION TIME 5 minutes
COOKING TIME 10 minutes

2½ cups very hot chicken or vegetable
    stock or miso soup
5 ounces dry udon, rice or egg noodles
1-inch piece gingerroot, peeled and
    finely grated
1 long red chili, very thinly sliced
    (seeded if you want a less fiery flavor)
2 large handfuls raw, shelled jumbo
    shrimp, thawed if frozen
2 handfuls vegetables, such
    as sugarsnap peas, baby corn cobs
    or chopped asparagus
1½ tablespoons soft light brown sugar
1½ tablespoons Thai fish sauce
4 scallions, very thinly sliced (optional)
juice of 1 lime
2 large handfuls cilantro and / or mint
    leaves

1 Put the stock in a saucepan over medium heat and bring to a boil. Add the noodles, ginger and chili, reduce the heat to low and simmer about 3 minutes until the noodles begin to soften.

2 Add the shrimp, vegetables, sugar and fish sauce. Simmer a few minutes longer until the shrimp and vegetables are cooked through.

3 Stir in the scallions, if using, the lime juice and herbs. Serve hot.

Leftovers are lovely jazzed up

nutty noodles

If you don't use the whole package of noodles and you have a block left over, they make a great quick lunch when you are on your own (or double up if you are not). Cook **1 portion udon, rice** or **egg noodles** according to the package directions. Drain and toss with **a drizzle chili** or **sesame oil**, **1 tablespoon oyster sauce**, **2 thinly sliced scallions**, **a squeeze lime juice** or **a splash rice vinegar** and **1 small handful chopped cilantro leaves**. Scatter **2 tablespoons chopped roasted peanuts** or **cashews** over and serve.

Having a package of gnocchi in the refrigerator or cupboard is a really good idea. It's a useful alternative to pasta and pretty much goes with anything. I'm always trying out different combos with stuff I find in my refrigerator, and this recipe has become a household favorite. Once you get the hang of this recipe, experiment with your own ideas—try swapping the broccoli for that leftover bag of spinach you always buy but sometimes forget to use.

Broccoli, Mushroom and Parmesan Gnocchi

MAKES 2 adult or 4 child portions
PREPARATION TIME 10 minutes
COOKING TIME 12 minutes

12 ounces to 1 pound 2 ounces bought
  gnocchi (depending on how hungry
  you are)
2 tablespoons olive oil
2 cups quartered or thickly sliced
  mushrooms
1 cup broccoli broken into small florets
2 garlic cloves, crushed
2 tablespoons water or white wine
  (optional)
4 tablespoons heavy or light cream
¼ teaspoon freshly grated nutmeg
a good squeeze lemon juice
¼ cup freshly grated Parmesan cheese
sea salt and freshly ground black pepper

1 Bring a pan of lightly salted water to a boil, add the gnocchi and return to a boil. Boil 2 minutes, or according to the package directions, then drain well.

2 Heat the oil in a large saucepan over medium heat, add the mushrooms, broccoli and garlic and cook 5 to 6 minutes until they are tender. If they start to stick to the pan or turn brown, add a splash of water or white wine, if you have some open, to create a little steam. Add the cooked gnocchi and fry 2 minutes, then add the cream and bring to a bubble.

3 Add the nutmeg, lemon juice and Parmesan and season lightly with salt and pepper. Stir the ingredients together a couple of minutes until well mixed. Serve hot.

I always buy exensive cheese in when we have friends come for a meal, and then I often find I have bought too much, so I concocted this deliciously filling recipe to use up some of that cheese.

Lemon Linguine with Walnuts, Spinach and Blue Cheese

MAKES 2 adult or 4 child portions
PREPARATION TIME 10 minutes
COOKING TIME 12 minutes

9 ounces dry linguine
½ cup walnuts
1 tablespoon olive oil
1 red onion, thinly sliced
finely grated zest and juice of 1 lemon
7 ounces frozen spinach, thawed
5 ounces blue cheese, such as
  Gorgonzola, dolcelatte, Danish blue
  or Stilton, cut into cubes
1 tablespoon extra virgin olive oil
sea salt and freshly ground black pepper

1 Bring a pan of lightly salted water to a boil, add the linguine and return to a boil. Boil about 10 minutes until just tender. Drain, reserving 2 tablespoons of the cooking water.

2 Meanwhile, heat a skillet over medium heat, add the walnuts and toast for a few minutes until they color lightly, tossing the pan gently. Tip them into a bowl.

3 Return the pan to the heat and add the olive oil. Add the onion and fry lightly for a few minutes until soft and lightly colored. Stir in the lemon zest and juice and the reserved pasta water and bring to a boil. Add the linguine and stir into the lemony juices about 1 minute. Add the spinach leaves, the blue cheese, walnuts and a good twist of black pepper. (Salt shouldn't be necessary, because the cheese is naturally salty.) Toss together until everything is well combined and the cheese is beginning to melt.

4 Drizzle the extra virgin olive oil over and serve hot.

Leftovers for a sweet treat
walnut and honey butter
Use any leftover walnuts to make this delicious butter. Lightly toast **½ cup walnuts** until lightly colored. Leave to cool, then pop them into a small blender and whiz with **7 tablespoons butter**, **a pinch ground cinnamon** and **3 tablespoons honey**. Use to spread over toast or warm baguettes, or to melt over the top of pancakes.

This is a lifesaver for those times when you can't be bothered to make much of an effort or you think you are out of provisions. When that happens, check your cupboards and refrigerator and you might be surprised. These are just suggestions for what you can do, but generally if you have onions, oil, beans and tomatoes as a base, you can add an array of ingredients depending on what you find. This is perfect for two adults served with baked potatoes, or on its own makes a hearty meal for one. If you also have chorizo or bacon in the refrigerator, fry it with the onions. A handful of fresh or frozen spinach can be stirred through at the end, or add chopped cilantro, basil or parsley leaves.

Pantry Bean and Tomato Stew with Baked Potatoes

MAKES 2 adult or 4 child portions
PREPARATION TIME 5 minutes
COOKING TIME 20 minutes

2 potatoes
1 tablespoon olive oil
½ white or red onion, sliced
1 garlic clove, crushed
½ cup white wine, red wine, sherry
  or beer (depending on what's open)
½ can (15-oz.) chickpeas or navy,
  borlotti, kidney, mixed or butter beans,
  drained , or even baked beans, with
  their sauce rinsed off
1 can (15-oz.) crushed tomatoes
1 bottled or canned roasted red bell
  pepper, sliced
1 handful ripe or green olives, pitted
a pinch dried chili flakes or cayenne
  pepper
sea salt and freshly ground black pepper
2 tablespoons butter, to serve

1 Heat the oven to 425°F.

2 Prick the potatoes a few times with a fork. Microwave on High 5 minutes, or until soft, then transfer them to the oven to crisp the skins.

3 Meanwhile, heat the oil in a skillet over low heat and fry the onion and garlic a few minutes until soft. Add the wine, sherry or beer. Bring to a boil, then reduce the heat and simmer about 5 minutes to cook away any alcohol (making this fine to serve to kids) and to reduce the quantity by half.

4 Stir in all the remaining ingredients and season lightly with salt and pepper. Bring to a simmer, then cook 5 to 8 minutes until the tomatoes are thicker.

5 Split open the potatoes and mix in the butter, then serve topped with the bean and tomato stew.

Serve these on their own as a snack or with tomato salsa and an arugula and avocado salad for a meal. A chunk of garlic bread on the side goes nicely, too. For added flexibility, once you have done your prep you can cook the fritters as and when you need them. The batter will keep in the refrigerator several hours.

Ricotta and Zucchini Fritters

MAKES 2 adult or 4 child portions
PREPARATION TIME 10 minutes
COOKING TIME 8 minutes each

1 cup plus 2 tablespoons ricotta cheese
2 zucchini, grated
⅓ cup peas, thawed if frozen, or corn
  kernels, rinsed if canned or thawed
  if frozen
⅔ cup self-rising flour
½ teaspoon paprika
1½ tablespoons chopped mint or basil
  leaves or snipped chives
finely grated zest of 1 small lemon
2 eggs, lightly beaten
olive oil, for frying
sea salt and freshly ground black
  pepper (optional)

1 Mix together the ricotta, zucchini, peas, flour, paprika, herbs, lemon zest and eggs. Season lightly with salt and pepper, if using. (The mixture can be kept in the refrigerator for a few hours or cooked straightaway.)

2 Heat about ½-inch oil in a heavy-based skillet over medium heat, add tablespoonfuls of the batter and cook 3 to 4 minutes on each side until golden brown and firm to touch. This quantity should make 12 fritters, so you will probably need to cook them in batches and keep the first ones warm in a low oven while you continue to cook the remainder.

3 Serve hot.

Lifesaver for pasta

pea pesto

It's worth thawing extra peas when you make the fritters so you can whiz up a vibrant, nutritious pesto to toss into pasta another day. This makes plenty for 2 adult and 2 child portions. Put **1¼ cups thawed frozen peas** in a food processor bowl along with **⅓ cup lightly toasted pine nuts**, **1 garlic clove**, **1 large handful chopped basil leaves**, **½ small handful chopped mint leaves**, **⅔ cup freshly grated Parmesan cheese**, **½ cup olive oil** and a little **sea salt** and **freshly ground black pepper**. Blend until smooth, adding a little water if the pesto seems too thick. Transfer to a bowl and cover with a thin layer of **oil** to help prevent discoloring. Use within 3 days. The pesto will thicken in the refrigerator so, when using, toss **1 to 2 tablespoons pasta cooking water** in with the pesto and pasta to loosen the sauce.

Stir-fries are the ultimate fast food, great for busy families, and most fish, meat and vegetable stir-fry combinations can be lifted with a sauce. These recipes can be made ahead and stored in a jar or sealed container in the refrigerator for about a week and used as and when you need them, so I've increased the serving quantities. Simply add any of these sauces to a stir-fry at the last minute to heat through.

Stir Crazy

EACH SAUCE MAKES 4 adult or 8 child
    portions
PREPARATION TIME 10 minutes
COOKING TIME 8 minutes

SWEET-AND-SOUR PINEAPPLE SAUCE

¾ cup plus 2 tablespoons pineapple
    juice
1 tablespoon cornstarch
1 tablespoon soy sauce
1 tablespoon rice vinegar or white wine
    vinegar
1 tablespoon tomato paste

1 Mix a little of the pineapple juice into the cornstarch to make a paste, then put all the ingredients into a small saucepan. Put over medium heat and bring to a boil, stirring occasionally, then reduce the heat and leave to simmer 1 to 2 minutes.

2 Stir the sauce into a stir-fry for the last minute of cooking to heat through.

COCONUT AND PEANUT SATAY

a drizzle sunflower oil
2 garlic cloves, crushed
¾ cup plus 2 tablespoons canned
    coconut milk
2 tablespoons crunchy or smooth
    peanut butter
1 teaspoon soy sauce
a pinch dried chili flakes
a squeeze of lime juice

1 Heat the oil in a saucepan over low heat, add the garlic and fry a few minutes until soft but not colored. Add the remaining ingredients and bring to a boil, then reduce the heat and leave to simmer 3 to 4 minutes.

2 Stir the sauce into a stir-fry for the last minute of cooking to heat through.

OYSTER, SCALLION AND GINGER SAUCE

2 tablespoons sesame oil
2-inch piece gingerroot, peeled and
    finely chopped or grated
2 garlic cloves, crushed
4 scallions, chopped
4 tablespoons oyster sauce
6 tablespoons orange juice
1 teaspoon rice vinegar or white wine
    vinegar

1 Heat the oil in a small saucepan, add the ginger, garlic and scallions and cook gently about 5 minutes. Add the remaining ingredients and bring to a boil, then reduce the heat and leave to simmer 2 to 3 minutes.

2 Stir the sauce into a stir-fry for the last minute of cooking to heat through.

This is a great recipe for your kids to make at home or for entertaining a group of their friends. You can dip just about anything in this delicious fondue (although maybe avoid toy cars and Barbie dolls!). To save time, buy bags of grated cheese, and for a more grown-up version, use wine instead of apple juice.

Under-21 and Over-21 Cheese Fondue

MAKES 2 adult or 4 child portions
PREPARATION TIME 10 minutes
COOKING TIME 5 minutes

FOR THE CHEESE FONDUE
½ cup apple juice or white wine
2 teaspoons cornstarch
1 small garlic clove, halved
⅔ cup grated Swiss or Gruyère cheese
⅔ cup grated cheddar cheese
¼ teaspoons freshly grated nutmeg

FOR DIPPING
you choose— virtually anything goes:
• cubes of crusty bread or breadsticks
• lightly cooked vegetables, such
  as broccoli, cauliflower, zucchini
  or baby corn cobs
• sticks of carrot, cucumber or bell
  pepper or cherry tomatoes
• grapes, sliced apple or pear
• cooked tortellini or other small filled
  pasta shapes

1 Mix 2 tablespoons of the apple juice into the cornstarch to make a paste. Pour the remaining apple juice into a saucepan and add the garlic. Bring the juice to a simmer over low heat, without letting it boil. Gradually stir in the cheese, leaving it to melt, then stir in the cornstarch paste. Cook a couple minutes until the fondue mixture is silky smooth and thick, stirring all the time. If you can find it, fish out the garlic clove, then finish by stirring in the nutmeg.

2 If you know the fondue will be eaten quickly, simply pour it into a warm bowl, or you can, of course, be more traditional and serve in a fondue pot—just make sure kids are careful with the naked flame. Or, if you have one, it can be served in a slow cooker set on low.

Leftovers for a family favorite
cauliflower macaroni and cheese
Warm any leftover cheese fondue with **a little milk** to loosen, then stir in the same quantity of **cooked mashed or pureed cauliflower**. Mix into **cooked macaroni**—you'll need about twice as much macaroni as cauliflower—scatter with a little **grated cheddar cheese**, transfer to a baking dish and broil until bubbling.

I have been cooking versions of this recipe for years, because it is so simple and flavorsome. It's great for throwing in the oven and tucking into with a green salad, ciabatta and a glass of wine. Kids love the flavors, too. For them, I just chop the cooked chicken into smaller pieces, and often use half wine and half stock. The dish freezes well and any leftovers make a great lifesaver meal for another day.

Mediterranean Baked Chicken and Rice

MAKES 2 adult and 4 child portions
PREPARATION TIME 15 minutes
COOKING TIME 45 minutes

4 boneless, skinless chicken breast
  halves
2 tablespoons olive oil
1 white or red onion, chopped
½ cup diced chorizo (optional)
1 red bell pepper, seeded and
  thinly sliced
2 garlic cloves, crushed
1¼ cups long-grain rice
2 cups plus 2 tablepsoons tomato puree
1½ cups white wine or chicken stock
1 teaspoon balsamic vinegar
8 to 10 sun-dried tomatoes in oil,
  roughly chopped
1¼ cups ripe or green olives, pitted and
  halved
1 handful of basil leaves, chopped
sea salt and freshly ground black pepper

1 Heat the oven to 350°F.

2 Cut 2 or 3 deep slits in the chicken pieces and season lightly with salt and pepper. Heat the oil in a Dutch oven, add the chicken and fry over high heat a couple of minutes on each side until brown. Remove the chicken from the Dutch oven and set aside.

3 Add the onion, chorizo, if using, red pepper and garlic to the pot and fry over medium heat 5 minutes, or until the onion is soft. Stir in the rice and, when it is coated in the oil, add the remaining ingredients. Season lightly with salt and pepper and bring to a simmer.

4 Return the chicken and any juices to the dish, pushing each piece into the sauce so they are partly covered. Cover the dish with a lid and bake 35 minutes, or until the chicken is cooked through and the sauce is rich, juicy and full of flavors. Serve hot.

Leftovers for a salad
chicken and rice salad

You can freeze individual portions of the above recipe, then thaw and reheat thoroughly within 3 months, or try this delicious salad. Put any leftovers from the main recipe in the refrigerator as soon as possible after they have cooled. The next day, cut any **chicken** into smaller pieces and stir it into the **cooked rice** with **olive oil** and **balsamic vinegar**. Toss in **salad leaves**, **diced cucumber** and **radishes** and some **sliced or diced avocado** to create a delicious salad.

This recipe ticks a lot of boxes: it can be frozen; it can feed the kids, then the adults, or it's a great family meal when you're all eating together; it can even be taken next door as a welcome-to-the-neighborhood gift; and it can be served with pasta, baked or mashed potatoes, rice or couscous. It's more versatile than a Swiss Army knife! This is another recipe that is worth making in a bigger quantity, so you can make Sausage Potpie (below) or freeze the leftovers for another meal.

Yummy Sausage Pot

MAKES 2 adult and 4 child portions
PREPARATION TIME 15 minutes
COOKING TIME 45 minutes

2 tablespoons olive oil
8 to 12 pork link sausages, left whole
  or chopped
1 onion, sliced or chopped
2 garlic cloves, crushed
1 red bell pepper, seeded and sliced
  or chopped
1 large carrot, peeled and grated
1½ cups chopped mushrooms
2¾ cups tomato puree
a pinch Italian herbs
1 teaspoon sugar
1 teaspoon balsamic vinegar
sea salt and freshly ground black pepper

1 Heat the oil in a large saucepan or Dutch oven, add the sausages and fry over medium-high heat about 10 minutes until brown.

2 Add the onion, garlic and red pepper, reduce the heat and fry about 5 minutes until the vegetables are beginning to become soft. Stir in the carrot and mushrooms and fry a couple minutes longer before adding the remaining ingredients. Bring to a boil, then reduce the heat, cover loosely with a lid and leave to simmer about 30 minutes until all the ingredients are cooked through and the sauce is thick. Season lightly with salt and pepper. (Anything not eaten straightaway will keep in the refrigerator a couple of days or can be frozen up to 3 months. Or, try my Sausage Potpie, below).

3 Serve hot.

Leftovers for a family pie

sausage potpie

Spoon the Yummy Sausage Pot into one large baking dish or individual dishes. If you don't have a huge amount of leftovers, bulk it out by mixing in **drained canned navy** or **butter beans**. Top the mixture with rolled out **puff** or **piecrust pastry dough**. Pierce a small hole in the top to let steam escape. Make an egg wash by mixing **1 egg yolk** with **1 tablespoon water** and brush it over the dough, or use **oil** or **milk**. Bake in an oven heated to 400°F 20 to 30 minues until the pastry is golden brown.

Kids will love the sweetness coming from the apricots and the aromatic cinnamon in this stew. For an authentic touch, serve it with plain couscous, or you can flavor the couscous with a little chopped mint, grated lemon zest and sliced green olives and serve it to friends as a dinner party main course. If you have any leftovers, you can make a Moroccan Shepherd's Pie (see below).

Moroccan Lamb Stew

MAKES 2 adult and 4 child portions
PREPARATION TIME 10 minutes
COOKING TIME 1½ hours

1 tablespoon olive oil
1 onion, thinly sliced
1 pound 10 ounces diced boneless
  lamb shoulder
2 teaspoons ground coriander
2 teaspoons hot paprika
3 teaspoons ground cinnamon
2 cans (15-oz.) crushed tomatoes
1¼ cups golden raisins
  or chopped apricots
1 handful cilantro leaves, chopped
sea salt and freshly ground black pepper
couscous, to serve

1 Heat the oil in a Dutch oven over medium heat, add the onion and fry a few minutes, or until starting to become soft. Increase the heat to high, add the lamb and cook a few minutes until brown, stirring continuously.

2 Add the spices, season to taste with salt and pepper and cook about 1 minute, stirring. Add the tomatoes and ¾ cup plus 2 tablespoons water. Bring to a boil, then reduce the heat to low, cover with a lid and leave to simmer 1 hour, stirring a couple of times during cooking.

3 After 1 hour, remove the lid, add the golden raisins and cook 20 to 30 minutes longer until the lamb is tender. (The dish can easily be left to cool and frozen at this point up to 3 months, then served another day. Or, you can make a Moroccan Shepherd's Pie out of any leftovers—see below.)

4 Scatter with the cilantro leaves and serve with couscous.

Leftovers for a taste of Morocco
moroccan shepherd's pie
Simply spoon any leftover **lamb** into a baking dish and stir in **frozen peas**, **green beans** or **fava beans**. Top with **mashed sweet potatoes** or a mix of **mashed carrots** and **white potatoes**. Dot with **butter** and bake in an oven heated to 400°F 20 to 30 minutes until the filling is hot and the topping is golden brown.

Here's an alternative recipe for that package of ground meat we all buy every week or we have kicking about in the freezer. Come rain or shine, this dish will please all the family with the rich delicious flavors in both the sauce and meatballs. It freezes well so I always make extra.

Meatballs with Olives

MAKES 2 adult and 4 child portions
PREPARATION TIME 15 minutes, plus
   10 minutes chilling (optional)
COOKING TIME 55 minutes

1 pound 2 ounces ground meat, such
   as beef, pork or lamb
1 onion, roughly chopped
2 garlic cloves, roughly chopped
1 egg, lightly beaten
2 tablespoons chopped mint leaves
   or 1 teaspoon dried mint
¼ teaspoon freshly grated nutmeg
3 tablespoons olive oil
1 large eggplant, finely diced
1 can (15-oz.) crushed tomatoes
⅓ cup red wine, water or stock
1 tablespoon red wine vinegar
1 teaspoon dried oregano
¼ teaspoon ground cinnamon
2 handfuls ripe olives, pitted and
   chopped
sea salt and freshly ground black pepper

TO SERVE
4 tablespoons plain or Greek yogurt
cooked rice or pita breads

1 Put the ground meat, onion, garlic, egg, mint and nutmeg in a food processor and season lightly with salt and pepper. Process until thoroughly combined. Using wet hands to stop the mixture sticking to your hands, shape the meatball mixture into balls the about size of a walnut in its shell. If you have the time, pop them in the freezer 10 minutes to firm up. (Alternatively, you can make the meatballs up to a day in advance and keep them in the refrigerator until you are ready to cook.)

2 Heat the oil in a large, shallow pan over medium-high heat, add the meatballs and fry a few minutes until they start to color, then remove them from the pan. Add the eggplant and fry a couple of minutes. Stir in the tomatoes, then the wine and wine vinegar. Add the oregano, cinnamon and olives, season lightly with salt and pepper and bring to a boil. Pop in the meatballs, reduce the heat, cover with a lid and leave to simmer gently 45 minutes until the sauce is thick and the meatballs are cooked through.

3 Drizzle a spoonful of plain or Greek yogurt over and serve with cooked rice or pita breads.

Leftovers for Greek-style lunch
meatball and tzatziki pitas

For a simple lunch, warm and split some **pita bread**, then fill with leftover **meatballs** (without too much sauce), either heated through or cold. Add **a few baby spinach leaves**, **a dollop tzatziki** and **pickled chilies**, then tuck in.

Bolognese sauce is such a household favorite that whenever I make it, I always make plenty and freeze the extra for when I need a quick dinner for the family—all I need to do then is thaw the sauce and boil some pasta. This is a really useful standby, because you can serve it with rice or baked potatoes, as well as simply boiled pasta, make it into lasagne, cannelloni or shepherd's pie, or use it to fill tortillas or crepes.

Good All-Around Bolognese Sauce

MAKES 6 adult and 6 child portions
PREPARATION TIME 10 minutes using
  Vegetable Starter Mix (see below)
  or 20 minutes from scratch
COOKING TIME 1¾ hours

2 tablespoons olive oil
½ recipe quantity Vegetable Starter Mix
  (see below)
2 pounds 4 ounces ground beef
1 cup plus 2 tablespoons red wine
2 beef bouillon cubes or 1 tablespoon
  concentrated beef stock
1 tablespoon chopped oregano leaves
  or Italian herbs
3 cups canned crushed tomatoes
2 tablespoons tomato paste
1 teaspoon sugar
1 teaspoon balsamic vinegar
¾ cup freshly grated Parmesan cheese
sea salt and freshly ground black pepper

FOR THE PASTA
about 3 ounces dry pasta per person

1 Heat the oil in a large pan over medium heat, add the vegetable starter mix and fry 5 minutes, or until the vegetables are starting to color. Stir in the ground beef, breaking it down with a wooden spoon so there aren't any large clumps. Cook over high heat until brown. Pour in the wine and boil 2 minutes, then add the remaining ingredients, except the Parmesan. Season lightly with salt and pepper.

2 Cover loosely with a lid and cook over low heat about 1½ hours, or longer if you have the time, until the sauce is rich and thick. (Alternatively, you can cook the sauce in an oven heated to 350°F the same length of time.) Leave the sauce to rest 10 minutes. (Any sauce you are not serving can be left to cool, then divided into portions to store in the refrigerator up to 3 days or in the freezer up to 3 months.)

3 While the sauce is resting, bring a large pan of lightly salted water to a boil, add the pasta and return to a boil. Boil about 10 minutes, or until just tender. Drain well.

4 Sprinkle the Bolognese with the Parmesan and serve with the pasta.

Lifesaver for the freezer

vegetable starter mix—soffrito

This is brilliant for using a glut of vegetables and makes a mega-convenient standby. It's based on the Italian *soffrito*: finely chopped aromatic ingredients softly fried and used as a base for soups, casseroles, tomato sauces, pasta sauces and chili con carne, to name just a few. Use these quantities as a guide: **2 large onions, 2 large carrots, 2 seeded red bell peppers, 2 zucchini, 8 garlic cloves, 4 celery sticks, 5 ounces mushrooms** (optional) and **4 tablespoons olive oil**. Finely chop the vegetables (I use a food processor) and fry in the olive oil until soft but not colored. If you get a lot of water coming out of them, just increase the heat so it evaporates. Either use some or all of the vegetables straightaway to start off a dish, or remove them from the heat and leave to cool, then divide and store in the refrigerator up to 3 days or label and store in the freezer up to 3 months. Thaw before using.

When I see braising steak on sale I often stock up so I can make this quick-and-easy, versatile recipe. I then make any leftovers into turnovers, which are perfect for the kids' meal the following day. Feel free to use diced lamb, if you prefer. You can replace the pickled pearl onions in the recipe with eight to ten peeled shallots, halved if large, or a large onion, thickly sliced, along with 1 tablespoon balsamic vinegar.

Simple Beef and Barley Casserole

MAKES 2 adult and 4 child portions
PREPARATION TIME 20 minutes
COOKING TIME 2 hours

1 pound 10 ounces braising steak, cut into small cubes
2 tablespoons all-purpose flour
5 ounces pickled pearl onions
2 celery sticks, cut into chunks
2 carrots, peeled and cut into chunks
2⅔ cups seeded, peeled and chopped butternut squash
⅓ cup pearl barley, rinsed well in cold water
2 tablespoons demerara sugar
2 teaspoons Worcestershire sauce
2 tablespoons tomato paste
1 large thyme sprig and 2 bay leaves, tied with a piece of string
2 cups plus 2 tablespoons beef stock
1 cup plus 2 tablespoons red wine
sea salt and freshly ground black pepper
cabbage or curly kale, to serve (optional)

1 Heat the oven to 315°F.

2 Toss the beef in the flour and season well with salt and pepper. This can either be done in a bowl or a large freezer bag. Put the meat in a large Dutch oven with all the remaining ingredients. Stir to mix everything together, then bring to a boil over high heat. Cover with a lid and bake 2 hours.

3 Serve the casserole just as it is or with buttery cabbage or curly kale.

Leftovers for lunchboxes
beef and barley turnovers

Take a sheet of **rolled puff** or **piecrust pastry dough** and cut out circles, as big or small as you like or depending on how much of the casserole you have left over. Brush the edges with **beaten egg** and spoon some **cold casserole** in the middle, making sure you don't use much of the sauce. Fold up the edges of the dough and pinch to seal. Pierce a hole in the dough of each turnover to let any steam escape while baking. Brush with egg, put on a greased cookie sheet and bake in an oven heated to 400°F 20 to 25 minutes until golden brown.

If you like the idea of very little dishwashing when you finally get the kids to bed so you can enjoy a meal with your partner, you're going to love this. It's a complete meal cooked all together in the oven (on a cookie sheet) in a parchment-paper bag. The best thing to do is to assemble the bags ahead (perhaps while the kids are eating their meal) and keep them in the refrigerator to cook later in the evening.

Baked Fish in a Bag with Tomatoes, Butter Beans and Chorizo

MAKES 2 adult or 4 child portions
PREPARATION TIME 10 minutes
COOKING TIME 20 minutes

1 can (15-oz.) crushed tomatoes
½ can (15-oz.) butter beans, drained and rinsed
⅔ cup pitted ripe olives
1 bottled or canned roasted red bell pepper, sliced
10 to 12 thin slices chorizo (about 1½ ounces), halved
2 large handfuls baby or young spinach leaves
2 fish fillets, such as cod, pollack, haddock or salmon, skinned
extra virgin olive oil, for drizzling
sea salt and freshly ground black pepper

1 Heat the oven to 425°F and put a large cookie sheet in the oven to heat.

2 Fold a 32-inch-long piece of parchment paper in half to make it double thickness, then fold in half again. Tightly fold together two of the edges to seal, creating a pouch and making sure there are not any gaps where the juices can escape during cooking. Repeat with another piece of parchment paper. (Alternatively, you can buy parchment paper bags from cookware stores that are ready to use.)

3 Divide the tomatoes between the packages, then do the same with the butter beans, olives, red pepper, chorizo and spinach. Season inside the bags with salt and pepper, then put the fish on top of the spinach. Season the fish and finish with a drizzle of extra virgin olive oil. Seal the open end of the bags by folding the edges over, leaving as much space inside the bags as possible for steam to circulate during cooking. (The packages can be prepared in advance and kept in the refrigerator several hours before cooking.)

4 Put the packages on the hot cookie sheet and bake 20 minutes, or until the fish is cooked through. When cooked, split open the packages and serve hot.

Make this recipe when you have a spare hour or so to leave it bubbling away, then serve it as a big family sit-down-together dish. (It can stretch to a few stray kids, too.) The chili can be frozen as individual portions to get out of the freezer as and when you need something to give your kids for a quick meal and something for the adults later in the evening (as can many of the recipes in this chapter). It's the recipe that keeps on giving. Keep it simple and serve with rice, but add some extras, such as grated cheese, sour cream, bought or Homemade Guacamole (see page 18) and wedges of lime.

Vegetable and Beany Gonzales Chili

MAKES 6 adult and 6 child portions
PREPARATION TIME 15 minutes
COOKING TIME 1 hour

2 tablespoons olive oil
1 large onion, chopped
2 red, green, yellow or orange bell
  peppers, seeded and diced
2 garlic cloves, crushed
2 zucchini, diced
2 cans (15-oz.) crushed tomatoes
1 can (15-oz.) red kidney beans, drained
2 teaspoons ground cumin
1½ teaspoons mild chili powder (or hot
  if you want added heat)
1 teaspoon ground cinnamon
2 teaspoons unsweetened cocoa powder
1 tablespoon chopped cilantro leaves
  (optional)
sea salt and freshly ground black pepper
cooked long-grain rice, to serve

1 Heat the oil in a large pan over low heat, add the onion and peppers and cook 5 minutes, or until beginning to become soft. Add the garlic and zucchini and cook 3 to 4 minutes longer.

2 Stir in all the remaining ingredients along with ½ cup water and season lightly with salt and pepper. Increase the heat and bring to a boil, then reduce the heat, cover loosely with a lid and leave to simmer 45 minutes, stirring a couple of times.

3 Scatter with the cilantro leaves, if using, and serve with rice.

Leftovers for Tex-Mex tacos
chili tacos and chili-baked wedges

If you want to serve this chili in a different way—perhaps for a lighter meal—then pop **1 handful shredded crisp lettuce**, such as iceberg, into a **taco shell**. Add a large **spoonful of the chili** and top with **grated cheese**. Serve with **sour cream** and / or **guacamole**, **lime wedges** and **hot-pepper sauce** for added heat, if you like.

Or, you could cook wedges of **potato** or **sweet potato** following the recipe on page 148, or use bought ones, if preferred. When cooked, transfer the wedges to individual baking dishes, or one large one if you are going to share, and spoon some of the **leftover chili** over. Scatter with **plenty of grated cheddar cheese** and pop into an oven heated to 400°F about 15 minutes until the chili is heated through and bubbling hot.

This Moroccan-inspired dish ticks so many boxes. It's healthy, comforting, full of flavor, quick and can easily be increased to serve more people, although these portions are fairly generous. What's more, the kids love the sweetness coming from the sweet potatoes and dried apricots. If you have extra sweet potatoes, they are great baked in a hot oven about 45 minutes, then served with a knob of butter and lots of freshly ground black pepper.

Chickpea and Sweet Potato Get-You-Out-of-a Stew

MAKES 2 adult and 4 child portions
PREPARATION TIME 10 minutes
COOKING TIME 1 hour

4 tablespoons olive oil
2 red or white onions, thickly sliced
6 garlic cloves, crushed
2 teaspoons ground cinnamon
2 teaspoons turmeric
2 teaspoons ground cumin
2 teaspoons paprika
1 teaspoon ground ginger
¼ teaspoon cayenne pepper
2 cans (15-oz.) crushed tomatoes
1 can (15-oz.) chickpeas, drained and rinsed
4 carrots, peeled and cut into large chunks
4 sweet potatoes, peeled and cut into large chunks
1⅓ cups ready-to-eat dried apricots, torn in half
2 large handfuls cilantro leaves, chopped
juice of 2 lemons

1 Heat the oil in a large Dutch oven or a tagine, if you have one. Add the onions and cook over low heat with the lid on about 10 minutes until they are soft and starting to color, stirring a couple of times during cooking. Stir in the garlic and spices and cook one minute or so before adding 1¾ cups water and all the remaining ingredients, except the cilantro and lemon juice.

2 Bring to a simmer and cover loosely with a lid. Leave to simmer up to 45 minutes until the sweet potatoes and carrots are tender.

3 Add the cilantro and lemon juice, stir through and serve.

This is a good standby meal in our house, as I always have peas and fava beans in the freezer, risotto rice in the cupboard and a few additional bits in the refrigerator. If you want to be a bit more fancy, you can use fresh peas, fava beans and other vegetables, such as green beans or asparagus. They'll just need cooking for a few minutes in boiling water before you add to the risotto. And if you've ever wondered what to do with leftover risotto, below is your answer. It's worth making this recipe just to try my Mozzarella and Risotto Primavera Cakes, below.

Baked Risotto Primavera

MAKES 2 adult and 4 child portions
PREPARATION TIME 10 minutes
COOKING TIME 25 minutes

2 tablespoons olive oil
1 tablespoon butter
1 large onion, chopped
3 garlic cloves, crushed
2 zucchini, diced
1½ cups carnaroli or arborio rice
4⅓ cups hot chicken or vegetable stock
grated zest of 1 small lemon
1 cup frozen peas, thawed
1 cup frozen fava beans or soybeans, thawed
3 tablespoons chopped chives, mint, basil or parsley leaves (or a mixture)
½ cup freshly grated Parmesan cheese
3 tablespoons mascarpone or cream cheese
sea salt and freshly ground black pepper

1 Heat the oven to 400°F.

2 Heat the oil and butter in a small Dutch oven over low heat, add the onion and garlic and fry 5 minutes, or until soft. Add the zucchini and rice and stir around until coated in the oil.

3 Stir in the stock and bring just to a boil, then cover with a lid and bake 15 minutes. If you are around, give it a stir halfway, but it's not essential. By now the rice will be just tender and most of the liquid absorbed. Stir in the peas and fava beans and return the Dutch oven to the oven 5 minutes.

4 Finally, when the risotto is ready, stir in the chopped herbs, lemon zest, Parmesan and mascarpone. Season lightly with salt and pepper and serve hot.

Leftovers Italian style
mozzarella and risotto primavera cakes

For every **1¼ cups leftover risotto**, mix in **2 tablespoons diced mozzarella** and **3 finely chopped sun-dried tomatoes**. Firmly shape into two cakes. Dip into **beaten egg** and then into **3 to 4 tablespoons fresh or dry bread crumbs**. Heat enough **olive oil** in a skillet to cover the bottom of the pan, add the risotto cakes and fry over medium heat 3 to 4 minutes on each side until golden brown and heated through. Drain on paper towels and serve.

These can be made and eaten straightaway or popped in the refrigerator and enjoyed within a couple of days. My mom used to make a similar dessert to this and hide a surprise in the bottom—chocolate buttons, pieces of fruit or little pieces of candy. I now realize she successfully used this as a way of encouraging me to eat up. Clever Mom!

Fruity Fools with Hidden Surprises

MAKES 2 adult or 4 child portions
PREPARATION TIME 10 minutes for soft fruit, or 15 minutes, plus cooling for hard fruits

⅓ cup heavy or whipping cream
1⅓ cups bought or Foolproof Homemade Custard Sauce (see page 114) or Greek yogurt
½ cup fruit puree (see method) or bought fruit compote or pie filling

FOR THE FRUIT PUREE
1⅔ cups hard fruit, such as chopped rhubarb or peeled, cored and chopped apples or pears
or 1⅔ cups soft fruit, such as berries, frozen smoothie mixes, seeded and peeled mango or pitted cherries, thawed if frozen
sugar, to taste

FOR THE SURPRISE
a few chocolate buttons, candies or pieces of fresh or dried fruit (optional)

1 To make a fruit puree, prepare your chosen fruit as necessary. If you are using hard fruit, they will need cooking. Put them in a pan over medium heat with 2 tablespoons water and bring to a boil, then reduce the heat to medium-low, cover with a lid and leave to simmer until the fruit is soft. Add sugar to taste and briskly stir or whiz in a blender until smooth. Leave to cool. If using soft fruit, put the fruit into a blender and whiz until smooth. Taste and add sugar, if needed.

2 To make the fools, beat the cream until it forms soft peaks. Fold in the custard sauce and the fruit puree, either until totally combined or creating a marbled effect.

3 Put a little surprise at the bottom of individual glasses or bowls, if you like, and spoon the fool over the tops. Either chill or eat straightaway.

Leftovers for iced treats
lollipop fools and fool ice cream
Rather than eating straightaway as a dessert, the fool mixture can be transformed into two very handy frozen treats.

To make Lollipop Fools, spoon the **fool** mixturre into lollipop molds and pop them in the freezer. The lollipops will last for a couple of months and are great for emergencies or cold treats on hot sunny days.

If you have an ice-cream machine, the **fool** mixture can be churned to make luscious, creamy, fruity Fool Ice Cream. Store in an old ice-cream container or a plastic box with a lid and it will be waiting for you in the freezer to tuck into and enjoy whenever the sun shines.

If there is ever a time when you want to say "well done"—whether it is for a good grade at school, doing well at a sport, cleaning up a bedroom or just for good behavior—an indulgent sundae is the best way to say it. Well, it works in my house.

Well-Done Mondaes to Fridaes

MAKES about 1 cup sauce
PREPARATION TIME 5 minutes
COOKING TIME 5 minutes

FOR THE HOT CHOCOLATE FUDGE SAUCE
3½ ounces dark chocolate, 70% cocoa
   solids, broken into small pieces
2 tablespoons unsweetened cocoa
   powder
⅓ cup golden syrup or light corn syrup
⅓ cup heavy cream
⅓ cup confectioners' sugar
½ teaspoon vanilla extract
a pinch salt

FOR THE SUNDAE
ice cream decorations, such as:
• crumbled meringues or cookies
• strawberries, sliced bananas or other
   favorite fruit
• whipped cream (this is a bit over the
   top but if they deserve it, then so be it!)
• edible space dust
• over-the-top decorations, such as
   wafers, paper umbrella, morello
   cherries

1 To make the fudge sauce, put the chocolate and cocoa powder in a large heatproof bowl. Rest the bowl over a pan of gently simmering water, so the bottom of the bowl does not touch the water. Stir occasionally until the chocolate melts. (Alternatively, you can do this in the microwave in 5-second bursts on Thaw or Low.) Remove the bowl from the heat and stir in all the remaining ingredients until smooth and well blended.

2 Layer up the sundae ingredients in tall sundae glasses or bowls and add whatever decorations you like. Spoon a little of the sauce over the ice cream and serve straightaway.

Lifesaver topping
hot chocolate fudge sauce
Once you have spooned some sauce over the ice cream, leave the rest to cool, then transfer to a glass jar with a lid and store in the refrigerator up to 4 weeks. You can serve it cold or gently heat whatever quantity you need.

Having a jar of homemade chocolate fudge sauce in your refrigerator is dangerous, of course, as it's very tempting to dip your finger into it every time you go into the refrigerator! But it will be a real hit spooned over an **ice cream sundae**. It's even great as a **crepe filling**, **poured over chocolate cake** or **pudding** or spread **on top of cupcakes**.

This is a midweek, restaurant-style dessert that certainly beats having plain fruit or yogurt at the end of your meal any day of the week. Of course, if you have a kitchen blowtorch, using that will be quicker than putting the desserts under the broiler, and adds drama to the recipe. The best bit of all is cracking the top of the brûlées with the spoon—the kids love it (and so do I!).

Fruit and Yogurt Brûlées

MAKES 2 adult or 4 child portions
PREPARATION TIME 5 minutes
COOKING TIME 2 minutes

3½ to 5½ ounces fresh soft fruit, such as plums, berries, banana or mango
a few drops vanilla extract, rosewater or orange flower water
1¼ cups Greek yogurt
¼ cup superfine sugar

1 If the fruit is large, cut it into smaller pieces and spoon it into the bottom of individual ramekins or other flameproof dishes. Mix the vanilla extract into the yogurt and spoon on top of the fruit. Smooth the surfaces, cover and keep in the refrigerator if not eating straightaway.

2 Heat the broiler to its hottest setting. Sprinkle the sugar over the yogurt in a thick, even layer. Put the ramekins onto a baking sheet and broil 1 to 2 minutes until the sugar melts and is golden and bubbling. Remove the desserts from the broiler and the sugar will set almost straightaway. Serve immediately.

How to make

super caramel

If you think your broiler just isn't powerful enough to make a decent caramel topping for the Fruit and Yogurt Brûlées, then fear not—it's very easy to make caramel separately in a pan. When you are ready to finish the crème brûlées, put the **¼ cup superfine sugar** in a small saucepan over low heat until it melts and turns a deep caramel color. Don't stir the sugar when it is caramelizing, but you can swirl the pan to guarantee even coloring. Pour or spoon a little of the caramel over each crème brûlée, then leave about a minute or so for the caramel to set before serving.

Crumbles make wonderful comfort food, especially when served with ice cream or custard sauce. For the filling, anything goes, but I've suggested some of the combinations we like best and created two different crumble toppings. Keep your favorite crumble mix in the freezer so you can simply make up your chosen filling and sprinkle the topping over.

Mix-and-Match Fruit Crumbles

MAKES 2 adult or 4 child portions, plus 10 adult portions
   of the crumble mixes for the freezer
PREPARATION TIME 10 minutes, using a made crumble mix
   or 15 minutes from scratch
COOKING TIME 20 minutes, or 30 minutes for apple and pear

SWEET CRUMBLE MIX

1 cup plus 2 tablespoons butter, diced
2½ cups all-purpose flour
1 cup plus 2 tablespoons packed soft
   brown sugar
1 cup rolled oats
a large pinch salt
2 teaspoons ground cinnamon, ground
   ginger or apple pie spice (optional)
1 cup slivered almonds, lightly crushed

1 Lightly rub together the butter and flour until the mixture resembles coarse, slightly chunky bread crumbs. Stir in the sugar, oats, salt, spice, if using, and almonds.

2 Reserve about 1½ cups for each two-person crumble. (Put the remainder in freezer bags in suitable quantities, label and freeze.)

GINGERSNAP CRUMBLE MIX

5 ounces gingersnap cookies
1 cup plus 2 tablespoons butter, diced
2½ cups all-purpose flour
1¼ cups sugar
 heaped ½ cup rolled oats
a large pinch of salt
2 teaspoons ground ginger

1 Put the cookies in a sandwich bag and crush with a rolling pin until you have large crumbs. Lightly rub together the butter and flour until the mixture resembles coarse, slightly chunky bread crumbs. Stir in the sugar, oats, crushed cookies, salt and spice.

2 Reserve about 1½ cups for each two-person crumble. (Put the remainder in freezer bags in suitable quantities, label and freeze.)

APPLE AND PEAR CRUMBLE

1 tablespoon butter
2 apples, peeled, cored and diced
2 pears, peeled, cored and diced
1 tablespoon sugar
1½ cups crumble mix of your choice
   (see left)
bought or Foolproof Homemade
   Custard Sauce (see page 114) or ice
   cream, to serve

1 Heat the oven to 400°F.

2 Melt the butter in a saucepan with the fruit, sugar and 1 tablespoon water. Cover and cook 5 minutes, or until slightly soft. Spoon the filling into baking dishes. Sprinkle your chosen crumble mix over the filling.

3 Bake about 20 minutes until bubbling and golden. Serve with custard sauce or ice cream.

CHERRY AND CHOCOLATE CRUMBLE

1 can (15-oz.) pitted cherries, strained
   with the syrup or juice reserved
2½ ounces dark chocolate, 70% cocoa
   solids, or milk chocolate, broken into
   small pieces
1½ cups crumble mix of your choice
   (see left)
bought or Foolproof Homemade
   Custard Sauce (see page 114) or ice
   cream, to serve

1 Heat the oven to 400°F.

2 Divide the cherries between two small baking dishes. Spoon enough syrup or juice over to half cover them. Sprinkle with the chocolate, then with your chosen crumble mix.

3 Bake about 20 minutes until bubbling and golden. Serve with custard sauce or ice cream.

FROZEN BERRY AND ORANGE CRUMBLE

grated zest of ½ orange
2 tablespoons sugar
2 cups frozen mixed berries, thawed
1½ cups crumble mix of your choice
   (see left)
bought or Foolproof Homemade
   Custard Sauce (see page 114) or ice
   cream, to serve

1 Heat the oven to 400°F.

2 Stir the orange zest and sugar into the fruit. Spoon into baking dishes. Sprinkle your chosen crumble mix over the filling.

3 Bake about 20 minutes until bubbling and golden. Serve with custard sauce or ice cream.

This is a great way to use up any leftover cooked rice. If you don't have any, however, it'll just take a little longer to make, or you can use bought cooked rice. The recipe also works with other fruit instead of bananas—try raspberries, strawberries, mango or pear. And, if you do not have any fresh fruit, it still tastes delicious just as a simple chocolate rice pudding.

Chocolate and Banana Rice Pudding

MAKES 2 adult or 4 child portions
PREPARATION TIME 5 minutes
COOKING TIME 20 minutes

1¼ cups cooked or leftover basmati or long-grain rice
2 cups plus 2 tablespoons milk, plus extra if required
1¾ ounces dark chocolate, 70% cocoa solids, broken into pieces
¼ cup sugar
2 bananas, peeled and sliced

1 Put the rice and milk in a nonstick saucepan. Bring to a boil over high heat, then reduce the heat to low and leave to simmer 20 minutes, or until thick, stirring occasionally.

2 Add the chocolate and sugar and stir gently until the chocolate melts and the sugar dissolves. Remove the pan from the heat and stir in extra milk, if necessary, if the mixture is too thick.

3 Either stir the bananas into the chocolate rice pudding and then spoon into a bowl, or arrange the bananas on top. Serve your rice pudding hot. (If you have any left over, leave it to cool, then chill and eat cold within a day.)

Leftovers for a treat
melting marshmallow risotto cakes

This is a little treat the kids will love—so much so you might want to make extra rice pudding just so you get one as well. Using wet hands to stop the mixture sticking to your fingers, roll the **leftover rice pudding** into balls, each about the size of a golf ball. Push your finger into the middle of each and push a **mini marshmallow** into the hole, then close the rice over the hole. Roll the balls in **beaten egg**, then in **crushed cookies**. Heat a little **butter** or **butter and oil** in a skillet, add the risotto cakes and fry gently until golden and fragrant, turning them frequently. Serve hot, warm or cold.

I have to admit, when chocolate is a must, these extremely quick-and-easy puddings are my guilty little pleasure. They are designed specifically for making in the microwave and are a true lifesaver. Stick to the basic pudding, or, for an additional treat, add a little surprise to them from the suggestions below. The cooking times are based on an 850-watt microwave. It's pretty amazing to see these puddings cook in a matter of minutes.

Lifesaver Speedy Chocolate Puddings

MAKES 2 adult or 4 child portions
PREPARATION TIME 5 minutes
COOKING TIME 2 minutes

FOR THE CHOCOLATE PUDDINGS
3 tablespoons sunflower, vegetable, grapeseed or peanut oil, plus extra for greasing
4 tablespoons self-rising flour
4 tablespoons sugar
3 tablespoons unsweetened cocoa powder
3 tablespoons milk
1 egg
½ teaspoon vanilla extract

SUGGESTIONS FOR THE EXTRA TREATS
choose your favorites, such as:
• 1 to 2 tablespoons chocolate chips
• a scattering of mini marshmallows
• 2 teaspoons jam
• finely grated orange zest
• 1 tablespoon chopped roasted hazelnuts or other nuts
• ½ banana, peeled and chopped

ice cream, to serve (optional)

1 Grease two microwave-safe teacups, small mugs or ramekins with oil. Mix together all the pudding ingredients until you have a smooth batter. then divide evenly between the prepared dishes. If you are adding an extra treat, gently stir it in.

2 Put in the microwave and cook on High 2 minutes.

3 Tuck in either as they are, or turn out into bowls and enjoy with a spoonful of ice cream, if you like.

Lifesaver dessert
speedy lemon syrup puddings
If it isn't chocolate you are craving but you want something deliciously comforting in a matter of minutes, you can easily use the basic recipe above and add additional flavors, such as **grated orange zest**, **ground ginger**, **ground cinnamon**, **almond extract** and so on. Here's how to make lemon syrup puddings: mix together **6 tablespoons self-rising flour** with **1 tablespoon sugar**, **2 tablespoons golden syrup** or **light corn syrup**, **3 tablespoons oil**, **3 tablespoons milk**, **1 egg** and the **finely grated zest of ½ lemon**. Cook as above in the microwave.

Every household that includes kids has to try these British classics—jam tartlets. These are so simple to make with the children of all ages. It doesn't matter if you use plain or fluted or large or small pans, you'll just get fewer tartlets with a larger pan. In the unlikely event you don't eat all the jam tartlets within a couple of days, don't let them go to waste —simply warm them through in the oven and serve with custard or transform into Jammy Apple and Almond Cakes (see below).

Jammy Apple Tartlets

MAKES 12 tartlets
PREPARATION TIME 5 minutes
COOKING TIME 15 minutes

melted butter, for greasing
about 12 ounces piecrust pastry dough, thawed if frozen
12 teaspoons jam, whatever flavor you like
1 apple, peeled, cored and thinly sliced
2 tablespoons shredded coconut or crushed slivered almonds
confectioners' sugar, for dusting (optional)
bought or Foolproof Homemade Custard Sauce (see page 114) or ice cream (optional), to serve

1 Heat the oven to 400°F. Use a pastry brush to brush the holes of a shallot tartlet or muffin pan with a little melted butter.

2 Using a cutter, cut out 12 circles of dough to fit the holes of the pan, then lightly press the dough into the holes. Put 1 teaspoon jam in each one, then lay the sliced apple on top. Scatter the shredded coconut or almonds over and dust each with confectioners' sugar, if you like.

3 Bake 12 to 15 minutes until the pastry is golden, the jam is bubbling and the apple is becoming golden.

4 While hot, carefully transfer to a wire rack and leave to cool. Serve warm or cold, dusted with more confectioners' sugar, and with custard sauce or a small dollop of ice cream, if you like.

Leftovers for almond cakes
jammy apple and almond cakes

If you don't eat all the tartlets, you can use them as a base for mini almond-flavored cakes. Line a muffin pan with paper cupcake cases, about twice as many as you have leftover tartlets. Roughly cut the **leftover tartlets** into ½-inch pieces and divide evenly among the cases. Beat together **7 tablespoons soft butter** and **½ cup superfine sugar**, then gradually add **3 beaten eggs** alternately with **1½ cups very finely ground blanched almonds** and **1 teaspoon almond extract**. This quantity will make 6 generous cakes, so adjust the quantities accordingly. Spoon the almond mixture into the cupcake cases and bake in an oven heated to 375°F about 25 minutes until risen and golden brown. Serve hot or cold.

THE BUSY WEEKEND

From family get-togethers to romantic meals for two ...

It's the weekend, which, when you think about it, is actually busier than Monday to Friday. You have clubs to go to, kids' parties to attend, more shopping to do, people to see, places to visit to broaden the minds of your children—basically, it's a crazy couple of days.

On top of all that (and no doubt much more), you love the idea of a fancier breakfast or brunch, you want to sit down and have a family lunch to catch up on the week's news and you'd very much like to have a candlelit meal for you and your other half on Saturday night. (Who says romance is dead?) Then there's the cake you must bake because your mom always made one to serve on the weekends and you need to live up to that!

In this chapter, you'll find the solutions to the juggling challenges the weekend throws up. I've been stress-testing them in my household since I started a family, so hopefully you should find something to suit your every need.

As with the other chapters, you'll find the quantities especially worked out so the family meals serve plenty for everyone—often with a bit left over to simplify the coming week—while the Saturday night recipes are just for you and your partner to share.

Even if your kids are not big on eating fruit or drinking a glass of milk on its own, they should enjoy one of these fruity options. In fact, most adults I know love them, too. Decorate with extra fruit, maple syrup or honey, if you like.

Milkshakes

EACH ONE MAKES 2 large or 4 small shakes
PREPARATION TIME 3 minutes

STRAWBERRY OR RASPBERRY SHAKE

1¾ cups milk
1⅓ cups strawberries or raspberries,
   hulled, if necessary
½ teaspoon vanilla extract
4 to 6 ice cubes
honey or maple syrup, to taste (optional)

1 Pour the milk into a blender. Add the fruit, vanilla extract and ice cubes and whiz 30 to 45 seconds until smooth. Add honey or maple syrup to taste, if you like.

2 Strain into glasses to remove any seeds or chunks of ice and serve.

BANANA AND PEANUT BUTTER SHAKE

1¾ cups milk
2 ripe bananas, peeled and roughly
   chopped
2 tablespoons peanut butter
4 to 6 ice cubes
honey, to taste

1 Pour the milk into a blender. Add the bananas, peanut butter and ice cubes and whiz 30 seconds, or until smooth. Add a little honey to taste.

2 Strain into glasses to remove chunks of ice and serve.

VANILLA AND MAPLE SYRUP SHAKE

1¾ cups milk
2 tablespoons maple syrup
1 teaspoon vanilla extract
4 to 6 ice cubes

1 Pour the milk into a blender. Add the maple syrup, vanilla extract and ice cubes and whiz about 15 seconds until smooth.

2 Strain into glasses to remove chunks of ice and serve.

If you're feeling a little rough around the edges from clinging onto your social life the night before and need help getting through the morning, a classic Bloody Mary should do the trick. If you're still feeling a little rough later on, use what tomato juice you have left and make a chilled Gazpacho Soup (see below).

Classic Bloody Mary

MAKES 2 glasses
PREPARATION TIME 5 minutes

½ cup less 2 tablespoons vodka
1¼ cups tomato juice
a good squeeze lemon juice
6 to 8 drops Worcestershire sauce
3 or 4 drops hot-pepper sauce
a pinch celery salt (optional)
freshly ground black pepper
ice

1 Measure the vodka and tomato juice into tall glasses.

2 Add the remaining ingredients to taste, stir together—and enjoy.

Leftovers for summer soup
gazpacho soup

If you have opened a carton or bottle of tomato juice, use any left over in all types of recipes. Try it as an alternative to milk in savory biscuits, instead of water in bread dough, in pasta sauces, casseroles and hot soups. Plus, you can turn it into a delicious chilled soup that is a summer favorite. Blend together **2 ripe tomatoes**, **¼ onion**, **¼ cucumber**, **½ red bell pepper**, **1 garlic clove**, **1 tablespoon extra virgin olive oil**, **1 teaspoon sherry vinegar** or **white wine vinegar**, **a dash hot-pepper sauce** and **1½ cups tomato juice** and season to taste with **sea salt** and **freshly ground black pepper** to give you a thick soup consistency. Serve chilled. This makes enough for 2 adult-size portions.

This is so easy to make—and if you have leftover cooked sausages, it's quick, too. If you don't—or you don't have time to cook them—just make ordinary French toast instead.

French Toast with Sausages

MAKES 2 adult and 2 child portions
PREPARATION TIME 5 minutes
COOKING TIME 15 minutes

sunflower oil, for frying
6 link pork sausages, split in half
  lengthwise
4 eggs
6 tablespoons milk
6 slices fresh white bread
ketchup, mustard, sweet chili sauce
  or barbecue sauce
3 tablespoons butter
sea salt and freshly ground black pepper

1 Heat a little oil in a large skillet over medium heat, add the sausages and fry about 5 minutes until lightly colored and cooked through.

2 Meanwhile, beat together the eggs and milk in a wide, shallow bowl and season lightly with salt and pepper.

3 When the sausages are cooked, lay them onto 3 slices of bread. Spread some of your chosen sauce over, then top with the other slices of bread. Press down firmly to seal. Lay the sandwiches in the egg mixture and leave to soak about 2 minutes. Carefully turn them over and soak 2 to 3 minutes longer until the egg mixture is absorbed.

4 Wipe out the pan with paper towels and put it over medium heat. Add the butter and, once it is bubbling, put the sandwiches in the pan. (If your pan isn't big enough to fit all 3 sandwiches, use just 1 tablespoon butter and cook one at a time.) Cook 3 to 4 minutes on each side until puffed up and golden, turning carefully with a metal spatula or pancake turner.

5 When the French bread sandwiches are cooked, halve one for the kids and serve with extra sauce of your choice.

According to my kids, this is what Woody and Jessie from *Toy Story* eat for breakfast every day to make them so strong. You can actually serve this dish any time of the day—I like it spooned over a baked potato when I'm in on my own, or when I'm home from work late and want something quick and hearty.

Cowboy Beans-on-Toast

MAKES 2 adult and 2 child portions
PREPARATION TIME 2 minutes
COOKING TIME 10 minutes

a drizzle olive oil
4 link pork sausages, skinned
2 cans (15-oz.) baked beans
barbecue sauce or smoked paprika, to taste
a couple drops hot-pepper sauce (optional)
wholewheat or white bread, toasted and buttered

1 Heat a skillet or saucepan over medium-high heat and add the oil, then break the sausages into the pan in chunks. Fry 5 minutes, or until the sausages are lightly colored and cooked through, breaking down any larger chunks of the sausages with a wooden spoon.

2 Add the baked beans and bring to a boil, then reduce the heat, stir in barbecue sauce to taste and cook a few minutes longer to thicken. Add hot-pepper sauce if you want a spicy kick.

3 Spoon onto buttered toast and off you go … Yeehaa!

Leftovers for sausage turnovers
cowboy turnovers

Use a sheet of **rolled puff pastry dough** or **piecrust dough** and cut out circles, as big or small as you like, or depending on how much of the cowboy beans you have left over. Brush the edges with **beaten egg** and spoon the cold filling into the middle of each. Add **grated cheese** if you want, too. Fold up the edge of the dough and pinch to seal. Pierce a hole in the the top of the dough to let any steam escape during baking. Brush with **egg**, put on a greased cookie sheet and bake in an oven heated to 400°F 20 to 25 minutes until golden brown.

Easy to prepare and delicious served with a toasted English muffin, this is really a dish for you and your partner, so you can add a splash of hot-pepper sauce for a kick, if you like. If you are using ham instead of the smoked salmon, it doesn't matter what type—prosciutto is particularly delicious. If you want to make this into more of a light lunch recipe, the addition of wilted spinach or a few fried sliced mushrooms—or both—in the bottom of the dishes makes it more substantial. And, of course, you can easily increase the quantities to serve more people.

Baked Eggs with Smoked Salmon or Ham

MAKES 2 adult portions
PREPARATION TIME 5 minutes
COOKING TIME 12 minutes

about 1 tablespoon butter, for greasing
2 to 4 slices smoked salmon or cooked or cured ham
2 eggs
2 tablespoons light or heavy cream
2 teaspoons snipped chives (optional)
1 tablespoon finely grated Parmesan cheese
sea salt and freshly ground black pepper
toasted and buttered English muffins or buttered toast, to serve

1 Heat the oven to 425°F and grease two individual baking dishes, such as ramekins, with butter. If you don't have any suitable dishes, two holes on a muffin pan will do.

2 Put the smoked salmon or ham into the dishes, pushing it to the edges to create a bowl shape. Break an egg into each one, then spoon the cream over. Season lightly with salt and pepper, scatter the chives over, if using, and finish with the cheese.

3 Put the dishes in the oven and bake 12 minutes, or until the egg whites are only just set and the yolks are still runny. The eggs will continue to cook once they are removed from the oven so don't be tempted to leave them in too long if you still want runny yolks.

4 Serve the eggs either in the baking dishes or turned out, with toasted buttered muffins or toast.

Forget heading for the same butter and jam on your weekend croissant—these are much more exciting combinations. The quantities listed for each recipe fill two croissants.

Baked Croissants

EACH ONE MAKES 2 croissants
PREPARATION TIME 5 minutes
COOKING TIME 5 minutes

FIG, GOAT CHEESE AND WALNUT CROISSANTS

2 croissants, split open
2 ripe figs, sliced
2 ounces crumbly goat cheese
1 small handful walnut pieces
honey, to taste

1 Heat the oven to 400°F.

2 Put the bottom half of the croissants on a cookie sheet. Put the figs on top, then scatter the cheese and walnuts over. Replace the tops. Bake the croissants 4 to 5 minutes until heated through. Drizzle with honey to taste. Leave the croissants to cool slightly, then serve.

RICOTTA, PROSCIUTTO, AVOCADO AND CHILI CROISSANTS

2 croissants, split open
4 tablespoons ricotta cheese
2 to 4 slices prosciutto
1 ripe avocado, pitted, peeled and sliced
a pinch dried chili flakes
sea salt and freshly ground black pepper

1 Heat the oven to 400°F.

2 Put the bottom half of the croissants on a cookie sheet. Spread with the ricotta and top with the prosciutto, avocado and chili flakes. Season lightly with salt and pepper. Replace the tops. Bake the croissants 4 to 5 minutes until heated through. Leave to cool slightly, then serve.

CHOCOLATE, BANANA AND ALMOND CROISSANTS

2 croissants, split open
3½ ounces dark chocolate, 70% cocoa
  solids, or milk chocolate, broken into
  small pieces
1 small banana, peeled and sliced
1 small handful toasted slivered
  almonds
confectioners' sugar, for dusting
  (optional)

1 Heat the oven to 400°F.

2 Put the bottom half of the croissants on a cookie sheet. Scatter most of the chocolate over and add all the banana and most of the almonds, then replace the tops. Finely chop the remaining chocolate and scatter over the croissants. Bake 4 to 5 minutes until they are crisp outside and oozing chocolate. Sprinkle with the remaining almonds, dust with confectioners' sugar, if you like, and leave to cool slightly, then serve.

Crepes don't have to be served just for dessert—they are also great fun to make with your kids for a family breakfast. Use a large skillet and add the minimum amount of batter so it very thinly covers the bottom of the pan. If you'd rather make the more familiar breakfast pancakes, however, take a look at my tip below that tells you how to adjust the basic recipe. Crepes are also a great way to make a meal out of leftovers. Good savory fillings include grated cheese, smoked salmon, cooked ham, cooked mushrooms and cooked spinach, to name just a few.

Foolproof Crepes or Pancakes

MAKES 8 to 10 crepes
PREPARATION TIME 5 minutes
COOKING TIME 4 minutes each

1 cup all-purpose or self-rising flour (use all self-rising flour for pancakes)
1 cup plus 2 tablespoons milk, plus exta if needed (use only 1 cup milk for pancakes)
1 egg
a pinch of salt
butter or sunflower oil, for frying

SUGGESTIONS TO SERVE
try some of these options:
• honey, maple syrup or jam
• Hot Chocolate Fudge Sauce (see page 64), chocolate spread or caramel sauce
• fresh fruit, such as berries or bananas
• grated lemon or orange zest and sugar
• yogurt
• ice cream … for breakfast? I know some of you will!

1 Put the flour, milk, egg and salt in a blender or food processor and mix together well. Alternatively, use a bowl and whisk until smooth. The consistency should be that of heavy cream for crepes, so add a little extra milk if you need to. (Cook straight away or chill for up to 24 hours until needed—loosen with extra milk if necessary.)

2 Heat a crepe pan or skillet over medium-high heat and add a small piece of butter or a trickle of oil until it covers the bottom of the pan. Add a spoonful of the batter, rolling the pan to spread it over the bottom thinly, and cook a couple minutes on each side until golden. Keep each crepe warm while you cook the remainder.

3 Serve with your chosen topping and enjoy.

Pancakes from scratch
breakfast pancakes
To make 12 to 14 light, fluffy pancakes the whole family will enjoy, follow the recipe above but use all self-rising flour and only 1 cup milk. Cook them in batches and keep warm in a low oven until all the batter is used.

Leftovers for a Sunday roast
yorkshire puddings
Any leftover batter can be used to make Yorkshire puddings to serve with roast beef. Keep the batter covered in the refrigerator. When you are ready to cook, heat the oven to 425°F. Put a good drizzle of sunflower oil in each hole of a muffin pan, and when the oven reaches the correct temperature put the muffin pan in 5 minutes, or until it gets hot. Quickly take the pan out and pour the **batter** into the holes, filling them halfway. Return the pan to the oven on the top shelf and cook 12 to 15 minutes until the Yorkshire puddings are risen and golden brown. Serve with a roast meal or as a snack topped with **baked beans** and **cheese**, or even as a dessert drizzled with **honey**, **maple syrup** and **lemon juice**.

We all need snack ideas to avoid resorting to the cookie jar, and this recipe is one to add to your armory. These are light, extremely great tasting and perfect for eating when you and the kids are on the go.

Savory Muffins

MAKES 12 muffins
PREPARATION TIME 15 minutes
COOKING TIME 20 minutes

butter, for greasing (optional)
⅓ cup pine nuts
2 cups self-rising flour
2 teaspoons baking powder
⅔ cup yellow cornmeal, polenta
   or semolina
1⅓ cups grated sharp cheddar cheese
1⅓ cups grated zucchini
2 eggs
1 cup plain yogurt
⅓ cup olive or canola oil
2½ ounces cooked ham, salami
   or chorizo, finely chopped
sea salt and freshly ground black pepper

1 Heat the oven to 350°F. Lightly grease the holes of the muffin pan, then press a 5-inch square of parchment paper into each hole, shaping the paper to fit by folding the sides. Alternatively, line a 12-hole muffin pan with paper cupcake cases.

2 Put the pine nuts in a dry, nonstick skillet over medium heat a few minutes, shaking and tossing the pan continuously until they start to turn golden brown. Tip them out onto a plate to cool. (Don't leave them in the pan or they will quickly burn.)

3 Mix together the flour, baking powder and cornmeal in a mixing bowl.

4 In a separate bowl, lightly mix together two-thirds of the cheese and all the remaining ingredients. Pour the wet ingredients into the dry ingredients and mix quickly and lightly to form a lumpy batter. (Over-mixing at this stage makes the muffins turn out heavy.) Spoon the batter into the prepared cases and scatter the remaining cheese over the tops. Put the pan in the oven and bake 20 minutes, or until risen and golden brown on the tops.

5 Leave the muffins to cool in the pan a few minutes, then transfer to a wire rack. Serve warm or cold.

Leftovers are delicious toasted

toasted muffins
The muffins are ideal for a picnic lunch served with tomato salsa, or for a weekday packed lunch. After a day or so, however, they become a little dry, but are delicious split in half and lightly toasted under the broiler, spread with **butter** or **cream cheese** and topped with **tomato salsa** or **a chutney**.

This recipe is hearty and flavorsome in the tradition of the Italian classic, the name of which means "big soup"—it's also quick and easy to make. You don't have to be strict about the ingredients you use—it really is a case of whatever vegetables you find in the refrigerator and whatever shape pasta you happen to have. Any leftovers can be reheated the next day with an extra splash of water if the soup is too thick (and a sneaky splash of dry sherry added when serving for the adults if it's been a tough day!).

Easy Minestrone Soup

MAKES 2 adult and 2 child portions
PREPARATION TIME 10 minutes
COOKING TIME 20 minutes

2 tablespoons olive oil
1 onion, chopped
2 to 4 smoked bacon slices, finely
   chopped (optional)
2 garlic cloves, crushed
2 celery sticks, thinly sliced
3 vegetables from your refrigerator,
   about 1½ cups chopped in total, such
   as a carrot, a small red bell pepper,
   a handful green beans, a small leek
   and a zucchini
3 cups hot vegetable stock
3 cups canned crushed tomatoes
   or tomato puree
2½ ounces dry linguine or spaghetti,
   broken into small pieces, or small
   pasta shapes
sea salt and freshly ground black pepper

TO SERVE
bottled green pesto (optional)
freshly grated Parmesan cheese

1 Heat the oil in a saucepan over medium heat, add the onion and bacon, if using, and cook 5 minutes, or until the onion is becoming soft. Stir in the garlic, celery and the chopped vegetables and cook about 5 minutes longer.

2 Add the stock, tomatoes and pasta and bring to a boil, then reduce the heat and slowly boil 10 minutes, or until the vegetables and pasta are tender. Season lightly with salt and pepper.

3 Ladle the soup into bowls, top with a spoonful of pesto, if you like, and serve sprinkled with grated Parmesan.

How to make

parmesan croutons

If you have a loaf of bread that's beyond its best, don't just give it all to the birds. Have a go at making cheese croutons to scatter over your weekend soup. To make enough for 4 adult-size portions, simply remove the crusts from **2 or 3 slices of bread** and cut each piece into about ½-inch cubes. Toss with **2 tablespoons olive oil** and **2 tablespoons finely grated fresh Parmesan cheese**. Tip onto a baking sheet and bake in an oven heated to 425°F 10 to 12 minutes, turning the cubes over a couple of times, until golden brown and crunchy. Leave to cool slightly.

Loaves of ready-to-bake French bread are a really convenient standby to have in your cupboard for those occasions when you've eaten all the bread at breakfast and haven't been shopping yet. You can adapt the recipe to use whatever different flavor combinations you like, such as mozzarella, roasted red bell pepper, pesto and prosciutto, or blue cheese, spinach leaves, avocado and bottled caramelized onions.

Baked French Bread with Your Favorite Fillings

MAKES 2 baguettes
PREPARATION TIME 10 minutes
COOKING TIME 15 minutes

2 loaves ready-to-bake French bread, white or wholewheat
1¾ cups grated sharp cheddar cheese
2 to 4 slices cooked ham, cut into pieces (optional)
2 to 4 scallions, finely chopped
2 to 3 tablespoons mayonnaise
3 sun-dried tomatoes, chopped
1 small handful basil leaves, torn into pieces
sea salt and freshly ground black pepper (optional)

1 Heat the oven to 400°F.

2 Split the bread loaves in half lengthwise and put the bottom of each one on a large piece of foil. Mix together the cheese, ham, if using, scallions and mayonnaise. Season lightly with salt and pepper, if you like. Spread the mixture over the bottom halves of the loaves, top with the sun-dried tomato and basil and put the other half of the loaf on top. Fold the foil up the sides of each loaf to cover it loosely, leaving the top open.

3 Put the foil packages directly onto the oven rack and bake 12 to 15 minutes, turning each loaf over halfway through. Remove the loaves from the foil and leave to cool slightly, then serve.

Kids love cheeseburgers and if you make your own, you know they are made with healthy ingredients. You can easily double the quantities to make more—so they are perfect for when your children invite their friends over for lunch or an after-school meal.

Cheeseburgers

MAKES 4 large or 6 small burgers
PREPARATION TIME 25 minutes
COOKING TIME 8 minutes

FOR THE BURGERS
1 pound 2 ounces ground beef
1 small onion, finely chopped
2 garlic cloves, crushed
2 teaspoons Dijon mustard
1 tablespoon Worcestershire sauce
1 egg yolk
oil, for brushing
sea salt and freshly ground black pepper
1 recipe quantity Perfect Coleslaw (see below), to serve (optional)

TO SERVE
burger buns or ciabatta rolls, split in half
¼ iceberg lettuce, shredded
3 tablespoons mayonnaise
1 or 2 tomatoes, sliced
4 to 8 slices of melting cheese, such as sharp cheddar, Swiss, Taleggio or blue cheese
1 red onion, sliced
gherkins, sliced (optional)
ketchup and / or mustard

1 Put all the burger ingredients, except the oil, in a bowl and mix well, preferably using your hands. Firmly shape into burgers. (Cook straightaway or chill until needed.)

2 When you're ready to cook the burgers, heat a griddle or skillet until it is really hot. Brush with a little oil, add the burgers and cook about 8 minutes, turning them every minute or so. Alternatively, cook on a hot barbecue over glowing white coals for the same amount of time. Constantly turning the burgers keeps them moist and guarantees they cook evenly.

3 While the burgers are cooking, lightly toast the burger buns or ciabatta rolls. Mix the lettuce with the mayonnaise and divide evenly onto the bottom halves of the buns, then top with the tomatoes. As soon as the burgers are cooked, top them with the cheese so it instantly starts to melt. Put the burgers on top of the tomatoes, then finish with red onion and gherkin, if using, ketchup and / or mustard. Serve with coleslaw, if you like.

How to make

perfect coleslaw

This has to be the perfect side dish to many meals, especially these cheeseburgers and the Speedy Steak and Pan-Fried Avocado Club Sandwich (see page 24). **Very thinly slice ½ red** or **white cabbage** and **1 small red** or **white onion** using the fine slicer blade on a food processor, a mandolin or a sharp knife. Then **coarsely grate 2 carrots** and mix with the cabbage and onion. In a separate bowl, mix together **4 tablespoons plain yogurt**, **2 tablespoons mayonnaise**, **1½ teaspoons Dijon mustard**, **1 tablespoon olive oil** and **1 tablespoon white wine vinegar**. Season with a little **sea salt** and **freshly ground black pepper**, then mix together the dressing and the vegetables. Keep in the refrigerator and use within 2 days. This makes enough for 2 adult and 2 child portions.

Get the kids involved in making these. They are fun and packed with flavor. Phyllo pastry dough is a great standby, and here I use it to wrap up a rice, shrimp and vegetable filling, but you can use your imagination to add other ingredients, depending on what you have in the cupboard or the refrigerator. Flaked canned tuna also works well, as does shredded cooked chicken or extra vegetables.

Shrimp Spring Rolls

MAKES 6 rolls
PREPARATION TIME 15 minutes
COOKING TIME 18 minutes

FOR THE SHRIMP FILLING
1½ cups cooked basmati rice (use bought cooked, leftovers or freshly cooked)
3½ ounces cooked shelled shrimp
1 cup peeled and coarsely grated carrot
½ red bell pepper, seeded and diced
1 to 1½ teaspoons sweet chili dipping sauce, plus extra to serve (or ketchup, if preferred)

FOR WRAPPING
6 sheets phyllo pastry dough, thawed if frozen, cut into twelve 9-inch squares
sunflower or vegetable oil, for brushing

1 Heat the oven to 425°F.

2 Mix together all the filling ingredients in a bowl. Lay a sheet of phyllo pastry dough on a cutting board or the countertop and brush lightly with oil. Put another sheet of dough on top and brush lightly with oil. Turn the square so one corner of the dough is pointing toward you.

3 Spoon about one-sixth of the filling onto the corner nearest you. Fold this corner toward the middle and tuck it under the filling. Fold the two outside corners into the middle so the package looks like an envelope. Brush lightly with oil, then roll up to look like a thick link sausage shape. Brush once more and put it on a nonstick cookie sheet. Repeat until you have made the remaining spring rolls. (Cook straightaway or chill until needed.)

4 Bake the spring rolls 15 to 18 minutes until they are light golden and crisp. Leave them to cool slightly, then serve with extra sweet chili dipping sauce or ketchup.

Leftovers with phyllo and chocolate
sweet sticks

If you had to cut rectangles of phyllo pastry dough into squares and you've ended up with **phyllo pastry dough trimmings**, they can be used to make chocolate or jam sweet sticks. Carefully spread **1 to 2 teaspoons chocolate and hazelnut spread** or jam in a fairly even layer on top of the dough, then roll up along the length of the dough, creating a thin stick shape. Brush with a little **oil** and dust with **confectioners' sugar**. Put on a nonstick cookie sheet and bake in an oven heated to 425°F about 8 minutes until crisp.

Quick and easy, this recipe uses ingredients you should be able to get from a local convienence store when the cupboards are bare, and it makes the perfect light meal with a salad for your weekend. If you don't have canned potatoes, boil salad potatoes and cut them into cubes, then continue with the recipe.

Pepper and Feta Frittata

MAKES 2 adult and 2 child portions
PREPARATION TIME 10 minutes
COOKING TIME 20 minutes

2 tablespoons olive oil
1 red or white onion, chopped
2 garlic cloves, crushed
3 cups drained and diced canned
    potatoes
2 bottled or canned roasted red bell
    peppers, cut into strips
1 cup frozen peas, thawed
1 small handful parsley leaves, chopped
6 eggs, beaten
1⅓ cups crumbled feta cheese
sea salt and freshly ground black pepper
mixed salad, to serve

1 Heat the oil in a flameproof 8-inch nonstick skillet over medium heat, add the onion and cook about 5 minutes until soft and just beginning to turn golden. Add the garlic and potatoes and continue to cook about 3 minutes until the potatoes are thoroughly heated through.

2 Stir the red peppers, peas and parsley into the beaten eggs and season lightly with salt and pepper, then pour the mixture into the pan and scatter the feta cheese over the top. Reduce the heat as low as possible and cook the frittata 10 to 12 minutes until it is almost set, carefully checking the underneath isn't burning by lifting the edge with a spatula.

3 Meanwhile, heat the broiler to high. Put the pan under the broiler a couple of minutes to cook the top of the frittata and give it a slightly golden appearance.

4 Slide the frittata onto a plate, cut into wedges and serve with a salad.

Leftovers for pasta

red pepper pesto

Use any of the leftover roasted red peppers to make a delicious pesto sauce. Lightly toast **⅓ cup pine nuts** in a dry skillet until just beginning to color. Tip them into a food processor and add **1 crushed garlic clove**, **1 large handful basil leaves**, **½ cup freshly grated Parmesan cheese**, **½ cup olive oil** and **1 roasted red bell pepper**. Season lightly with **sea salt** and **freshly ground black pepper** and blitz until smooth. Use straight away or pour into a clean jar, cover with a little extra oil, seal with a lid and store in the refrigerator up to a week.

Aarrrrgh! It's lunchtime, you're all hungry and your plan was to go grocery shopping after lunch, so there's nothing in the kitchen. Well, have a dig around in the refrigerator for an onion, grab a potato and get some vegetables out of the freezer and you're ready to start cooking.

Frozen Vegetable Soup

MAKES 2 adult and 2 child portions
PREPARATION TIME 10 minutes
COOKING TIME15 minutes

2 tablespoons butter
1 small onion, chopped
2 garlic cloves, crushed
1 small Idaho potato, peeled and diced
1 bay leaf (optional)
2 cups plus 2 tablespoons hot vegetable
   or chicken stock
2 cups frozen vegetables (peas, carrots,
   corn kernels—whatever you have)
2 tablespoons mascarpone, cream
   cheese or light or heavy cream
sea salt and freshly ground black pepper
crusty bread, to serve

FOR THE FLAVORINGS
if you are using a single vegetable,
it is easy to add extra flavors,
for example:
• cauliflower: add 1 teaspoon Dijon
   mustard to the soup and stir through
   grated cheddar cheese at the end
   rather than the mascarpone, cream
   cheese or cream
• peas: fry a few bacon slices with the
   onion, and add 2 tablespoons chopped
   mint leaves at the end
• broccoli: add a good grating
   of nutmeg, and stir in an extra
   2 tablespoons cream cheese at the
   end, or use blue cheese if you have
   any, which is particularly nice

1 Melt the butter in a large saucepan over medium heat and when it is bubbling, add the onion, garlic, potato and bay leaf, if using. Cover with a lid and cook over medium heat 10 minutes, stirring a couple of times.

2 Add the stock and bring to a boil. Stir in the vegetables, return the stock to a boil and boil 5 minutes, or until the vegetables are tender. Remove the bay leaf, if you used one, and blitz the soup with a hand blender or in a blender until it is smooth.

3 For a creamy finish, stir in the mascarpone and season lightly with salt and pepper. Stir in any extra flavorings, if you like.

4 Serve hot with crusty bread to dip in.

Leftovers for another day
garlic croutons

There are no rules for making this kind of soup, just use whatever you have to hand, ingredients you want to use up or random items from the vegetable drawer. Just don't use too many strongly flavored vegetables—taste as you go along. It's quite likely you'll end up with more than you need for one sitting, but you'll certainly not waste it. Serve it for lunch the next day, perhaps sprinkled with some **freshly grated Parmesan cheese** or **garlic croutons**, made by quickly frying **cubes of bread** in **hot oil** with a **crushed garlic clove**. Or, simply leave the soup to cool, pack it in plastic boxes in suitable quantities, label and put in the freezer so it is there as a save-the-day soup for another time.

Making pizzas with the kids is great fun. This is a basic Margherita pizza, but you can add any topping you like. My favorite is nuggets of sausagemeat, broccoli florets and dried chili flakes, but ricotta cheese, prosciutto, sun-dried tomatoes and olives comes a close second. The kids love decorating their own by making faces with chunks of vegetables.

Pizza Art

MAKES 2 large or 4 small pizzas
PREPARATION TIME 20 minutes, plus
  30 minutes rising (optional)
COOKING TIME 10 minutes

FOR THE PIZZA DOUGH
2½ cups white bread flour, plus a little
  extra for dusting
1 teaspoon quick-rising dry yeast
1 teaspoons salt
1 tablespoon olive oil

**FOR THE TOMATO AND MOZZARELLA
  TOPPING**
⅔ cup Tomato Sauce (see below)
  or tomato puree
1 handful basil leaves, torn or roughly
  chopped
9 to 12 ounces mozzarella, torn into
  pieces
olive oil, for drizzling
plus any of your favorite toppings
  as extras

1 Put the flour, yeast and salt in bowl and make a well in the middle. Pour in the oil and ¾ cup plus 2 tablespoons warm water and bring the ingredients together with a wooden spoon or your hands until you have a soft, fairly wet dough. Turn out the dough onto the countertop dusted with flour and knead a good 5 minutes, or until smooth and elastic. Alternatively, mix everything together in a mixer with a dough hook.

2 If you have the time, put the dough in a clean, lightly greased bowl and cover with a piece of greased plastic wrap. Leave the dough in a warm place about 30 minutes. It's not essential to do this for a thin-crust pizza but it does make a lighter crust.

3 Heat the oven to 475°F. Put two baking sheets in the oven on separate shelves to heat and lightly flour two other baking sheets.

4 Knead the dough quickly if you have left it to rise, then divide it into two or four pieces. Roll out each piece thinly, then put it on the cold baking sheets. Spread the tomato sauce over the dough and scatter with the basil and mozzarella. Add any other toppings of your choice. Drizzle the pizzas with olive oil and put the cold baking sheets in the oven on top of the heated ones. Bake the pizzas 8 to 10 minutes until the crusts are golden and crisp, then serve the pizzas cut into wedges.

Lifesaver for your pantry
tomato sauce

Use this sauce for serving with broiled meat and fish, as a pizza topping, with pasta or gnocchi, as a soup base, a dip or a salsa with chili. Simmer **3 cups canned crushed tomatoes**, **3 tablespoons olive oil**, **2 crushed garlic cloves**, **1 teaspoon sugar**, **1 teaspoon balsamic vinegar**, **2 tablespoons chopped basil leaves** (optional) and **sea salt** and **freshly ground black pepper** in a pan 30 minutes, stirring occasionally, or until rich and thick. Use straightaway or cool and store in the refrigerator up to a week. To keep, spoon into sterilized jars and seal loosely with a lid. Put them in a roasting pan lined with a folded dish towel and pour in ¾ inch hot water. Put in an oven heated to 315°F 25 minutes, then remove from the pan and seal tightly. Store in a cool, dark place and use within 6 months. Once open, store in the refrigerator and use within 3 days.

There's no racing about and getting in a flap with this roast dinner—everything you need is cooked in one pan. If you are lucky enough to have any leftovers, then you really must try the Roast Chicken Potpie recipe, below.

Simple Slow-Roast Chicken Dinner

MAKES 2 adult and 2 child portions
PREPARATION TIME 15 minutes
COOKING TIME 3 hours

4-pound free-range or organic chicken
3 tablespoons butter, soft
1 butternut squash, halved, peeled, seeded and cut into wedges
2 large carrots, peeled and cut into large chunks
2 or 3 parsnips, peeled and cut into chunks (central core removed if tough)
1 garlic bulb, halved through the middle
2 or 3 rosemary, thyme or sage sprigs
2 cups plus 2 tablespoons chicken stock
½ cup white wine
1 tablespoon cornstarch
2 tablespoons heavy cream or sour cream (optional)
sea salt and freshly ground black pepper

1 Heat the oven to 315°F.

2 Put the chicken in a large roasting pan and smear the butter over the chicken and the bottom of the pan. Put the vegetables, garlic and herbs around the chicken. Pour ½ cup of the stock and the wine over. Season lightly with salt and pepper. Cover the pan with a piece of aluminum foil and roast 1 hour. Remove the foil and baste the chicken and vegetables with the pan juices, turning the vegetables. Return the pan to the oven and roast, uncovered, 1 hour longer.

3 Increase the oven temperature to 425°F. Baste the chicken and vegetables, then roast 30 minutes longer until the chicken is golden and the juices from the chicken run clear when the thickest part of the thigh is pierced with a skewer.

4 Remove the chicken from the roasting pan and leave it to rest, loosely covered with foil. Return the pan to the oven 15 minutes longer to crisp the vegetables. Transfer the vegetables to a serving plate.

5 Drain off the fat and put the roasting pan over high heat. Add the remaining stock and any resting juices from the chicken and scrape any sticky residue from the bottom and sides of the pan. Stir 1 tablespoon water into the cornstarch, then stir this into the pan and bring to a boil. Cook 2 minutes, stirring continuously. Finish by stirring in the cream, if you like. Carve the chicken and serve with the vegetables.

Leftovers make delicious potpies

roast chicken potpie

Use any leftover chicken, or any cooked meat and vegtables, to make a pie. Blend **1 tablespoon butter** and **1 tablespoon all-purpose flour** in a pan over low heat, then whisk in **1 cup hot stock** until smooth. Simmer a few minutes, then stir in **2 tablespoons heavy cream**, **1 teaspoon mustard**, **a squeeze lemon juice** and **2 tablespoons chopped parsley leaves** and season with **sea salt** and **freshly ground black pepper**. Add **1½ cups each chopped cooked meat and veg**. Divide between one large or two individual baking dishes. Roll out **9 ounces puff pastry dough** and moisten the edges to seal to the top of the dish(es). Cut a hole in the top and brush with **egg**, **milk** or **oil**. Put on a hot cookie sheet and bake in an oven heated to 400°F 30 minutes, or until golden brown and piping hot.

A delicious dish for busy families, this is a great recipe to make on a Sunday night when you've been out for the day and need something to literally throw together. It's also just as delicious eaten cold as hot, so you can enjoy any leftovers the next day with a green salad and crusty bread.

Roasted Spanish(ish) Chicken Thighs

MAKES 2 adult and 2 child portions
PREPARATION TIME 15 minutes
COOKING TIME 1 hour

8 to 12 boneless, skinless chicken thighs (depending on their size)
2 red bell peppers, seeded and cut into wedges
1 large onion, cut into 8 wedges
3 cups salad potatoes, scrubbed and halved if large
4 garlic cloves, lightly crushed
1 lemon, cut into wedges
3 tablespoons olive oil
20 thin slices chorizo, halved
1 large handful pitted green olives, plain or stuffed with pimientos or anchovies
5 ounces cherry or baby plum tomatoes
sea salt and freshly ground black pepper

1 Heat the oven to 425°F.

2 Put the chicken, red peppers, onion, potatoes, garlic, lemon and oil in a large roasting pan and toss all the ingredients together so they are coated in oil. Season lightly with salt and pepper. Put the pan over high heat on the stovetop and stir everything together for a couple minutes to get some heat into the ingredients, then place the pan in the oven and roast 30 minutes, turning all the ingredients around in the pan halfway through.

3 Add the remaining ingredients, return the pan to the oven and roast 30 minutes longer, turning the ingredients a couple of times for even cooking, until everything is juicy, golden and delicious. The juices from the chicken should run clear when the thickest part of the thighs are pierced with a skewer. Serve hot.

I love sweet potatoes for the change they make from ordinary white potatoes, so here's an alternative sausages and mashed potato dish. It's really easy with the added incentive that the dishwashing is minimal.

Sticky Sausages with Sweet Potatoes and Peppers

MAKES 2 adult and 2 child portions
PREPARATION TIME 15 minutes
COOKING TIME 1 hour

12 pork link sausages
2 pounds sweet potatoes, peeled and
    cut into wedges
2 red onions, cut into wedges
4 rosemary sprigs
2 red, yellow or orange bell peppers,
    seeded and thickly sliced
3 tablespoons olive oil
sea salt and freshly ground black pepper

FOR THE STICKY MIX
3 tablespoons light or dark soft brown
    sugar
1 tablespoon wholegrain mustard
1 tablespoon white or red wine vinegar
1 tablespoon orange or pineapple juice

1 Heat the oven to 425°F.

2 Put all the main ingredients, apart from the sticky mix, in a roasting pan and toss together. Put the pan in the oven and roast 30 minutes, giving everything a stir halfway through.

3 Stir together all the sticky mix ingredients and pour into the pan, giving all the ingredients a good stir so they are coated. Return the pan to the oven and roast 30 minutes longer, turning all the ingredients a couple of times, until the sausages are cooked through, sticky and lightly colored. Remove the rosemary sprigs and serve hot.

leftovers for a filling salad

sausage and couscous salad

It is unlikely there will be any of this dish left over, because it is exceptionally difficult to resist seconds. If there are leftovers, however, you can use them to make a salad to serve for lunch the following day, either at home or in a packed lunch to take to school or work. Simply leave any leftovers to cool, then cut everything into bite-size pieces. Measure **½ cup couscous** into a bowl, pour **7 tablespoons boiling water** over and stir together. Leave to stand 10 minutes, stirring occasionally, until cool. Stir in **a dash of olive oil** and **a sprinkling of lemon juice**, then add the **sausages** and you are ready to go.

This hearty casserole is ideal to serve as an alternative to a roast meal when you are short of time. All you have to do is throw all the ingredients into a Dutch oven, pop it in the oven and leave it to cook. The only other effort required is to whiz together the dumpling ingredients in a food processor and add them to the Dutch oven toward the end of the cooking time.

Lamb and Red Currant Casserole with Rosemary Dumplings

MAKES 2 adult and 4 child portions
PREPARATION TIME 20 minutes
COOKING TIME 2½ hours

FOR THE CASSEROLE
1 pound 10 ounces boneless lamb shoulder, diced
heaped 3 tablespoons all-purpose flour
2 large onions, thickly sliced
½ rutabaga, peeled and cut into bite-size pieces (optional)
2 celery sticks, sliced
2 carrots, peeled and sliced
3 tablespoons red currant jelly
2 tablespoons red wine vinegar
2 teaspoons Worcestershire sauce
2 tablespoons tomato paste
1¾ cups red wine
1 cup less 2 tablespoons lamb or beef stock
sea salt and freshly ground black pepper
cabbage or curly kale, to serve

FOR THE DUMPLINGS
⅔ cup self-rising flour, plus extra for dusting
1½ cups fresh white bread crumbs
5 tablespoons butter, diced
2 teaspoons Dijon mustard
1 tablespoon finely chopped rosemary leaves
1 extra-large egg, lightly beaten

1 Heat the oven to 315°F.

2 Put the lamb and flour in a bowl or large plastic freezer bag and toss well, making sure all the lamb is coated in the flour. Put the lamb and all the remaining casserole ingredients in a large Dutch oven, mix well and bring to a boil over high heat. Cover with a lid and place in the oven 2 hours, or until the sauce starts to become thick.

3 Meanwhile, make the dumplings. Put the flour, bread crumbs and butter in a food processor and blitz until the mixture resembles bread crumbs. Add the mustard, rosemary and egg and season lightly with salt and pepper. Blitz briefly until the mixture forms a fairly moist dough. Using floured hands to stop the mixture sticking to you, divide the dough into 8 equal portions and roll them into balls.

4 After the casserole has been cooking 2 hours, remove the Dutch oven from the oven and uncover. Put the dumplings on top of the lamb and sprinkle a few flakes of salt on top of each one. Return the Dutch oven to the oven, uncovered, and continue cooking 30 minutes longer, or until the dumplings are golden and the casserole is rich and thick. Serve the casserole just as it is or with buttery cabbage or curly kale.

Leftovers for something different
red currant lamb and green bean potpie
Mix any **leftover casserole** with **blanched green beans** and spoon into a large or individual baking dishes. Top with **puff pastry** or **piecrust pastry dough**, pierce a hole in the top and brush with **milk** or **a beaten egg**. Bake in an oven heated to 400°F 25 to 30 minutes until golden.

The beauty of this recipe is that you can make the turnovers small for young children or big, using larger salmon fillets, for adults. You can also make these using phyllo pastry dough, layering three sheets together and brushing with melted butter between each.

Gone-in-a-Puff Salmon Turnovers

MAKES 2 adult and 2 child portions,
depending on the size of the fillets
PREPARATION TIME 15 minutes
COOKING TIME 20 minutes

¾ cup mascarpone or cream cheese
2 tablespoons chopped dill
or snipped chives
1 teaspoon Dijon mustard
finely grated zest of 1 lemon
10 scallions, thinly sliced
4 salmon fillets, whatever size suits
you all
13 ounces puff pastry dough, thawed
if frozen
1 egg yolk
1 tablespoon milk
sea salt and freshly ground black pepper

TO SERVE
seasonal vegetables or salad
cooked potatoes, tossed in butter and
chopped mint (optional)

1 Heat the oven to 425°F. Line a cookie sheet with parchment paper or use a nonstick baking sheet.

2 Mix together the mascarpone, dill, mustard, lemon zest and scallions, and season lightly with salt and pepper. Spread over the top of the salmon fillets.

3 Cut the dough into four pieces large enough to wrap around each piece of salmon. Put the fillets on the dough and fold over the remaining dough to make a neat package. Trim off any excess, if necessary. Cut a couple of holes in the top of each turnover for any steam to escape during baking, then put them on the prepared baking sheet. (You can cook them straightaway or chill until needed.)

4 When ready to cook the turnovers, mix together the egg yolk and milk to make an egg wash and brush it over the top of each. Bake the turnovers 20 minutes, or until the fish is cooked through and the pastry is golden brown.

5 Serve hot with vegetables or a salad, and cooked potatoes tossed in butter and chopped mint, if you like.

Lifesaver for the freezer
marinated five-spice salmon
When you have fresh salmon fillets or cutlets (or any other fish fillets or cutlets for that matter) you plan on freezing, coat them in a flavorsome marinade first. That way all you need to do is thaw the fish in the refrigerator on a day you want a quick-and-easy evening meal that's not out of a package. For **1 fillet** or **cutlet**, mix together **½ teaspoon Chinese five-spice powder**, **2 teaspoons soy sauce** and **1 tablespoon honey**. Put the marinade in a freezer bag with the fish and seal tightly. Move the fish around so it is evenly coated, then label the bag and put it in the freezer. When you're ready to use, thaw the fish and broil, bake, fry or even barbecue it until it is cooked through and the flesh flakes easily. Add **a squeeze of lime** and serve with **noodles** or **rice** and **stir-fried vegetables**.

A humble sheet of puff pastry or piecrust dough is a perfect canvas for a variety of toppings, depending on what you and your family like, are in the mood for or you have sitting in the refrigerator. Here are three recipes that are favorites in my Madhouse, but feel free to be as creative as you like and come up with your own ideas for good combinations of flavors.

Three Ways with Simple Savory Tarts

EACH ONE MAKES 2 adult and 4 child portions
PREPARATION TIME 15 minutes
COOKING TIME 25 minutes

SMOKED SALMON AND LEEK TART

1 tablespoon olive oil, plus extra
   for drizzling
2 tablespoons butter
1 large leek, thinly sliced
13 ounces piecrust or puff pastry dough
   sheets, thawed if frozen and rolled out
   if necessary
1 cup plus 2 tablespoons ricotta cheese
2 eggs, lightly beaten
2 garlic cloves, crushed
1 small handful tarragon, chervil
   or parsley leaves, finely chopped
finely grated zest of 1 lemon
7 ounces hot-smoked salmon or smoked
   trout, flaked
1 tablespoon freshly grated Parmesan
   cheese
sea salt and freshly ground black pepper
green salad or vegetables, to serve

1 Heat the oven to 400°F and line a cookie sheet with parchment paper.

2 Heat the oil and butter in a skillet over low heat, add the leek and cook gently a few minutes, or until soft. Remove the skillet from the heat.

3 Lay the dough on the prepared cookie sheet, score a ¾-inch border with a sharp knife and prick the middle part of the dough several times with a fork.

4 Mix together the ricotta, eggs, garlic, your chosen herb, salt and pepper. Spread over the dough, inside the border, then top with the leeks, lemon zest and salmon. Finish by scattering the Parmesan over, add a drizzle of olive oil and brush the dough edges with oil. Bake the tart 25 minutes, or until the pastry is golden brown and the filling softly set.

5 Serve hot with a green salad or vegetables.

SPINACH, PEPPER AND PINE NUT TART

1¾ cups frozen spinach, thawed
1 cup plus 2 tablespoons ricotta cheese
2 eggs, lightly beaten
2 garlic cloves, crushed
¼ teaspoon freshly grated nutmeg
13 ounces piecrust or puff pastry dough
    sheets, thawed if frozen and rolled out
    if necessary
3 bottled or canned roasted red bell
    peppers, cut into strips
¼ cup freshly grated Parmesan cheese
⅓ cup pine nuts
olive oil, for drizzling
sea salt and freshly ground black pepper
green salad or vegetables, to serve

1 Heat the oven to 400°F and line a cookie sheet with parchment paper.

2 Squeeze the excess water out of the spinach and mix together with the ricotta, eggs, garlic and nutmeg. Season lightly with salt and pepper.

3 Lay the dough on the prepared cookie sheet, score a ¾-inch border with a sharp knife and prick the middle part of the dough several times with a fork. Spread the spinach and ricotta mixture over the dough, inside the border, then scatter the red peppers, Parmesan and pine nuts over. Drizzle with a little olive oil and brush the edges of the dough with oil. Bake the tart 25 minutes, or until the pastry is golden and the filling softly set.

4 Serve hot with green salad or vegetables.

TOMATO, ASPARAGUS AND PROSCIUTTO TART

13 ounces piecrust or puff pastry dough
    sheets, thawed if frozen and rolled out
    if necessary
1 cup plus 2 tablespoons ricotta cheese
2 eggs
1 small handful basil leaves, shredded
2 garlic cloves, crushed
¼ cup freshly grated Parmesan cheese
9 small tomatoes, halved
8 to12 asparagus spears, cut into 2-inch
    pieces
6 to 8 slices prosciutto, torn
olive oil, for drizzling
sea salt and freshly ground black pepper
green salad or vegetables, to serve

1 Heat the oven to 400°F and line a cookie sheet with parchment paper.

2 Lay the dough on the prepared cookie sheet, score a ¾-inch border with a sharp knife and prick the middle part of the dough several times with a fork.

3 Mix together the ricotta, eggs, basil, garlic and half of the Parmesan. Season lightly with salt and pepper. Spread over the dough, inside the border. Top with the tomatoes, asparagus and prosciutto, as rustic or neatly as you like. Scatter the remaining Parmesan over and drizzle with olive oil. Brush the edges of the dough with oil. Bake the tart 25 minutes, or until the pastry is golden and the filling softly set.

4 Serve hot with green salad or vegetables.

Whether you are a meat eater or not, this will disappear quckly. It's hearty, nutritious and straightforward to prepare. I always make this quantity, as it's a great lunch dish for an extended family, with any leftovers to serve the following day, or to put in the freezer. My advice is to use fresh lasagne sheets, because you can simply cut them to fit your dish, rather than getting frustrated by trying to snap dry sheets—no matter how hard you try, they never break where you want.

Rich Vegetable Lasagne

MAKES 4 adult and 4 child portions
PREPARATION TIME 25 minutes
COOKING TIME 1½ hours

2 red bell peppers, seeded and cut
    into chunks
1 eggplant, cut into chunks
2 zucchini, cut into chunks
4 whole garlic cloves, unpeeled
3 tablespoons olive oil
1½ cups halved cherry tomatoes
1½ cups tomato puree, ideally flavored
    with basil
2 tablespoons bottled red or green
    pesto
1 handful ripe olives, chopped (optional)
7 ounces fresh lasagne sheets
4 ounces mozzarella, grated or torn into
    small pieces
¼ cup freshly grated Parmesan cheese
sea salt and freshly ground black pepper

FOR THE BÉCHAMEL SAUCE
3 tablespoons butter
1 bay leaf
½ cup less 1 tablespoon all-purpose
    flour
2 cups plus 2 tablespoons milk
¼ teaspoon freshly grated nutmeg

1 Heat the oven to 400°F.

2 Put the red peppers, eggplant, zucchini and garlic in a roasting pan and toss with the oil. Put the pan in the oven and roast the vegetables 25 minutes. Add the cherry tomatoes and turn them gently in the oil. Return the pan to the oven and continue roasting 15 to 20 minutes longer until the vegetables are cooked through and light brown.

3 Meanwhile, to make the béchamel sauce, melt the butter in a saucepan with the bay leaf over medium heat. Once it is bubbling, stir in the flour and cook a couple minutes, stirring all the time. Gradually add the milk and bring to a boil, still stirring. Reduce the heat and stir until the sauce is thick, then leave to simmer over very low heat 5 minutes, stirring occasionally. Remove the bay leaf, add the nutmeg and season lightly with salt and pepper.

4 Once the vegetables are roasted, remove the garlic cloves and squash the cooked garlic to a paste. Stir this paste into the tomato puree along with the pesto and olives, if using. Pour the tomato puree into the roasting pan with the vegetables, season lightly with salt and pepper and stir to combine.

5 Reduce the oven temperature to 350°F.

6 Spoon one-third of the vegetable mixture into the bottom of a large baking dish that is suitable to serve from. Top with a layer of lasagne sheets, then drizzle one-third of the béchamel sauce over. Repeat so you have three layers of lasagne, finishing with the béchamel sauce. Scatter the mozzarella and Parmesan over. (You can prepare the lasagne up to this stage, leave to cool and chill until needed.) Put the baking dish on a cookie sheet and and bake 45 minutes, or until golden brown and bubbling. Remove from the oven and leave to rest 10 minutes, then serve.

An old-fashioned favorite, I just had to include a sticky toffee pudding in the book, and my family love this banana version. The portions are deliberately generous to make sure there's plenty left over to enjoy the rest of the week.

Sticky Toffee and Banana Pudding

MAKES 2 adult and 2 child portions
PREPARATION TIME 15 minutes
COOKING TIME 30 minutes

FOR THE BANANA PUDDING
6 tablespoons butter, soft, plus extra
   for greasing
2 cups pitted and chopped dates
1 cup plus 2 tablespoons brewed tea
1 teaspoon baking soda
1 cup sugar
2 eggs, beaten
1½ cups less 2 tablespoons self-rising
   flour
2 ripe bananas, peeled and mashed
1 teaspoon apple pie spice
ice cream, to serve

FOR THE STICKY TOFFEE SAUCE
½ cup soft light or dark brown sugar
5 tablespoons unsalted butter
½ cup heavy cream

1 Heat the oven to 350°F and grease an 8-inch square baking dish.

2 Put the dates and tea in a small saucepan and bring to a boil and boil 3 to 4 minutes until soft, then stir in the baking soda.

3 Using an electric mixer, beat together the butter and sugar until light and creamy. Stir in the eggs, flour, bananas, apple pie spice and date mixture until well combined. Pour into the prepared baking dish, transfer to the oven and bake 40 to 45 minutes until the top is just firm to the touch.

4 Meanwhile, to make the sauce, put the brown sugar, butter and cream in a saucepan over low heat and simmer until the sugar dissolves and the sauce is a light toffee color. (Both the pudding and sauce can be gently reheated and served within a few days. Alternatively, a slice of pudding can be popped into lunchboxes or enjoyed with a cup of coffee.)

5 Once cooked, pour the warm sticky toffee sauce over the pudding and serve with ice cream or custard sauce (see below).

How to make
foolproof homemade custard sauce
Making your own custard sauce is very quick and simple, and using a little cornstarch guarantees a smooth result. To make 2½ cups sauce, pour **2⅓ cups milk** or **half-and-half** and **¾ teaspoon vanilla extract** into a nonstick saucepan over medium-low heat and bring a simmer. Meanwhile, whisk together **4 egg yolks**, **2 teaspoons cornstarch** and **¼ cup less 1 tablespoon sugar** with a balloon whisk until well blended. Gradually pour the hot milk into the eggs, whisking as you pour. Return the mixture to the pan and stir over low heat until it is thick, making sure it doesn't boil. Serve hot or pour into a sauceboat or bowl, cover with plastic wrap directly on the surface to prevent a skin forming, and leave to cool. Once completely cool, refrigerate and use within 3 days.

P.S. If you like the idea of Chocolate Custard Sauce simply stir **1¾ ounces dark chocolate**, 70% cocoa solids, into the hot custard until it melts and is combined.

A household favorite when I was growing up, this is now fast becoming a favorite with my kids. Maybe this can become your Madhouse signature dish?

Saucy Chocolate and Orange Pudding

MAKES 2 adult and 2 child portions
PREPARATION TIME 20 minutes
COOKING TIME 40 minutes

**FOR THE CHOCOLATE AND ORANGE
    PUDDING**
½ cup butter, soft, plus extra
    for greasing
½ cup sugar
finely grated zest of 1 large orange
½ teaspoon vanilla extract
a pinch salt
⅔ cup self-rising flour
2 tablespoons unsweeted cocoa powder
2 eggs
2 tablespoons milk
ice cream (optional), to serve

FOR THE CHOCOLATE SAUCE
½ cup soft light or dark brown sugar
2 tablespoons unsweetened cocoa
    powder

1 Heat the oven to 375°F and grease a 5-cup baking dish with butter.

2 Using an electric mixer, beat together the butter, sugar, orange zest, vanilla extract and salt until light and creamy. In a separate bowl, sift together the flour and cocoa powder, then add one spoonful to the butter mixture along with 1 egg. Beat well, then repeat with the other egg. Finally, mix in the remaining flour and cocoa powder, along with the milk to give a soft dropping consistency. Transfer to the prepared dish and smooth the surface with a spatula.

3 Now for the wow factor. Mix together the soft brown sugar, cocoa powder and 1¼ cups just-boiled water until the cocoa dissolves. Pour over the top of the pudding, then bake the pudding 40 minutes until the top is springy to the touch.

4 Spoon the chocolate and orange baked top layer into bowls, revealing the rich and delicious sauce at the bottom of the dish and spoon it over. Serve the pudding as it is or with ice cream, if you like.

Leftovers for a sweet herb flavor
dill and orange butter
If you have used the orange zest, you'll obviously want a way to use up the juice. Put the **juice of 1 orange** in a small saucepan over medium heat and simmer until you have just 2 tablespoons remaining. Beat into **½ cup soft butter** with **1 tablespoon chopped dill**. Season lightly with **sea salt**. Spoon onto a piece of wax paper and twist the ends together to form a link sausage shape. Store in the refrigerator a few days and slice off individual pieces when needed. Use to flavor fish while it steams or bakes, or add a slice on top of cooked fish to melt over the surface.

Need a quick dessert to quite literally throw together to finish off your family meal before the kids race off and find better things to do than be sociable with their parents? All you need for this is fruit (fresh or thawed), bought meringues and heavy cream. Then add more madness and jazz it up with anything you find in the cupboards.

Madhouse Mess

MAKES 2 adult and 2 child portions
PREPARATION TIME 10 minutes

1¼ cups heavy or whipping cream, Greek yogurt, sour cream, crème fraîche or ice cream (thawed to a dolloping consistency)
3 or 4 bought meringue nests or 2 or 3 handfuls mini meringues
2 cups soft fruit, thawed if frozen and cut into small pieces if necessary: virtually anything goes, such as berries, bananas, ripe pears or canned fruit, such as peaches, apricots, pears or cherries, grapes, mango and so on
2 tablespoons jam, such as raspberry, strawberry or cherry (optional)

TO JAZZ IT UP
choose your favorites from:
• chocolate chips
• cake sprinkles
• chocolate candies
• mini marshmallows
• edible space dust
• or anything else your kids can get their hands on

1 Put the cream, or whatever you are using, in a large mixing bowl. If you are using cream, then whisk to form soft peaks. Crumble in the meringues, then throw in the fruit. Using a large spoon, fold everything together, then swirl in the jam, if using—if the fruit you are using is naturally sweet, the jam won't be necessary.

2 Spoon into dishes and, if you're jazzing up your Madhouse Mess, scatter the chosen treat over and tuck in.

Ice cream in an instant—your kids will be amazed! Don't worry if you don't have frozen cherries, you can use frozen raspberries or mixed berries instead. You might need to add a little extra honey for sweetness. Alternatively, to make a banana ice cream, peel and chop four bananas. Freeze them in a plastic freezer bag for a couple of hours, then use as below instead of the cherries.

Magic Ice Creams

EACH ONE MAKES about 2 cups
PREPARATION TIME 5 minutes

CHERRY ICE CREAM

2⅓ cups frozen pitted cherries
⅔ cup bought or Foolproof Homemade Custard Sauce (see page 114)
⅓ cup heavy cream
2 to 3 tablespoons honey

1 Put all the ingredients in a food processor and whiz until you have a soft, smooth, creamy ice cream.

2 Either serve straightaway or transfer to a container with a lid and store in the freezer.

NUTTY BANANA AND CHOCOLATE ICE CREAM

4 ripe bananas, peeled, cut into chunks and frozen
⅔ cup bought or Foolproof Homemade Custard Sauce (see page 114)
⅓ cup heavy cream
3 tablespoons chocolate and hazelnut spread
chopped toasted hazelnuts, for sprinkling

1 Put all the ingredients, except the chopped nuts, in a food processor and whiz until you have a soft, smooth, creamy ice cream.

2 Either serve straightaway scattered with chopped nuts or transfer to a container with a lid and store in the freezer and scatter the nuts over when you serve.

MANGO ICE CREAM WITH COOL COCONUT SPRINKLES

2 cups frozen mango chunks
⅔ cup bought or Foolproof Homemade Custard Sauce (see page 114)
⅓ cup heavy cream
2 to 3 tablespoons honey

FOR THE COCONUT SPRINKLES
a few handfuls shredded coconut
different colored food coloring

1 For the sprinkles, put 1 handful of shredded coconut in a freezer bag and add a drop of food coloring. Seal with air in the bag and shake like crazy until the coconut is colored. Tip onto a plate to dry for a few minutes. Repeat with as many colors as you like.

2 To make the ice cream, put all the ingredients in a food processor and whiz until you have a soft, smooth, creamy ice cream.

3 Either serve straightaway scattered with colored coconut sprinkles or transfer to a container with a lid and store in the freezer. (Leftover sprinkles can be stored in an airtight container for weeks.)

I've always wondered how to make fruit leather, partly due to my kids loving it and also because buying it is expensive. I saw a recipe in the *River Cottage Handbook No. 2, Preserves* by Pam Corbin, had a play around and came up with this recipe. It's delicious, great to make with the children—and not bad for you, either.

Blueberry and Apple Fruit Strips

MAKES a sheet about 8 x12 inches
    to cut into strips
PREPARATION TIME 10 minutes
COOKING TIME 30 minutes on the stovetop,
    then 6 to 8 hours in a very low oven

1⅔ cups blueberries
heaped 2 cups peeled, cored and
    chopped cooking apples
5 tablespoons honey
juice of ½ lemon
¼ teaspoon vanilla extract

1 Put all the ingredients in a saucepan and bring to a boil over medium heat. Reduce the heat and leave to simmer 25 to 30 minutes until you have a thick puree, stirring occasionally.

2 When the puree is almost ready, heat the oven to 150°F and line a large cookie sheet with parchment paper (not wax paper) or a silicone sheet.

3 Press the puree through a strainer, pushing as much of the puree through as possible. Thinly spread the puree over the cookie sheet into a rectangle about 8 x 12 inches, as evenly as you can. Put the cookie sheet into the oven and leave for 6 to 8 hours until the puree becomes firm and dry.

4 Carefully peel the fruit strip away from the parchment paper and hold it up to the light. It looks amazing! Cut it into strips and roll into coils. (The fruit strips can be kept a couple of months at room temperature in an airtight container.)

Never throw away overripe bananas, because it's so easy to make this quick-to-whiz-together and ever-popular bread with them instead. You can leave out the preserved ginger, if it's not your thing. If you don't have a bread pan, make Banana and Ginger Muffins instead. Simply line a 12-hole muffin pan with paper cupcake cases and spoon in the batter. Reduce the baking time to 18 to 20 minutes until the muffins are golden brown and springy to the touch. Cool on a wire rack, then dust with confectioners' sugar to serve.

Banana and Ginger Loaf

MAKES a 9- x 5-inch loaf
PREPARATION TIME 10 minutes
COOKING TIME 1 hour

¾ cup butter, soft, plus extra
   for greasing
2 really ripe bananas, peeled and
   roughly chopped
4 tablespoons roughly chopped
   preserved ginger
2 eggs
1 cup less 2 tablespoons soft light brown
   sugar
1¼ cups plus 2 tablespoons self-rising
   flour
½ teaspoon vanilla extract
a pinch salt
confectioners' sugar, for dusting

1 Heat the oven to 315°F. Grease a 9- x 5-inch bread pan with butter and line with parchment paper.

2 Put all the ingredients in a food processor and whiz until smooth. Spoon the batter into the prepared pan and smooth the surface with the back of your spoon. Bake the banana and ginger loaf 1 hour, or until the top is golden brown and the loaf is baked through. To test, insert a skewer into the middle: if the loaf is baked, the skewer will come out clean. If not, return the loaf to the oven 5 to 10 minutes longer.

3 Leave the loaf to cool in the pan 10 minutes, then turn out, peel off the paper and leave to cool on a wire rack. Dust with confectioners' sugar and serve warm or cold.

If you want to make a cake instead of cupcakes, grease and line two 7-inch round cake pans and divide the batter evenly between them. Bake the cakes 20 to 25 minutes until risen and just slightly springy. Leave the cakes to cool in the pans 5 minutes, then turn out, peel off the paper and leave to cool completely on wire racks. Sandwich the cakes together with the frosting, then frost the top.

Carrot Cupcakes with Cream Cheese Frosting

MAKES 12 cupcakes
PREPARATION TIME 20 minutes
COOKING TIME 20 minutes

FOR THE CARROT CUPCAKES
⅔ cup canola or sunflower oil
½ cup packed soft light brown sugar
2 eggs, lightly beaten
3½ tablespoons golden syrup or light corn syrup
1½ cups less 1 tablespoon self-rising flour
1 teaspoon ground cinnamon
¼ teaspoon ground allspice
½ teaspoon ground ginger
1 teaspoon baking soda
2 cups peeled and finely grated carrots
½ cup golden raisins
¼ cup shredded coconut

FOR THE CREAM CHEESE FROSTING
5 tablespoons unsalted butter, at room temperature
5 tablespoons cream cheese
finely grated zest of 1 orange, plus extra to decorate
2 cups confectioners' sugar, sifted

1 Heat the oven to 350°F and line a 12-hole muffin pan with paper cupcake cases or lightly grease a silicone cupcake tray.

2 Using an electric mixer, in a large bowl, whisk together the oil, sugar, eggs and syrups until combined. Mix in all the remaining cake ingredients, then spoon the batter into the cupcake cases.

3 Bake the cupcakes 20 minutes, or until nicely risen and firm but springy when lightly pressed. Leave the cupcakes to cool in the pan 5 minutes, then transfer to a wire rack to cool.

4 To make the frosting, using an electric mixer, beat the butter until smooth. Add the cream cheese and orange zest and beat another minute or so. Add half of the confectioners' sugar and mix together on a low speed. Add the remaining confectioners' sugar and mix until the frosting is light and creamy. Chill until needed.

5 When the cakes are completely cool, spread or pipe the frosting on top, sprinkle with extra orange zest and serve. (These delicious cupcakes keep well for a few days in an airtight container in a cool place, remaining nice and moist.)

Lifesaver for a speedy cake
cream cheese frosting
The cream cheese frosting recipe freezes really well, so it is well worth making a double quantity and storing it in the freezer. Then, if you ever need to tart up a bought cake, muffins or cupcakes, you have a homemade frosting to hand. As an alternative to orange zest, you can flavor it with the **grated zest of 1 lemon**, **1 teaspoon ground cinnamon** or **ground ginger**, or **seeds from 1 vanilla bean**, or even color it **pink** and add **a few drops rose water**.

These muffins are fun, yummy (who doesn't love a marshmallow?) and irresistible when still warm from the oven. And, if you do happen to have any left over a day or so later, don't throw them out, because they can be used to make a delicious granola for breakfast.

Raspberry-Marshmallow Muffins

MAKES 12 muffins
PREPARATION TIME 15 minutes
COOKING TIME 25 minutes

2⅓ cups self-rising flour
½ cup plus 1 tablespoon sugar
1¼ cups fresh or thawed raspberries
¾ cup mini marshmallows
⅔ cup milk
½ cup butter, melted
1 egg, beaten

1 Heat the oven to 350°F and line a 12-hole muffin pan with paper cupcake cases or lightly grease a silicone muffin tray.

2 Put the flour, sugar, raspberries and marshmallows in a mixing bowl and lightly mix together so the raspberries are coated in flour. This prevents the raspberries from sinking to the bottom of the muffins while they are baking.

3 Mix together the milk, butter and egg, then gently mix the liquid mixture into the flour mixture. Spoon the batter into the muffin cases or tray and bake the muffins 25 minutes, or until risen and golden.

4 Leave the muffins to cool in the pan a few minutes, then transfer to a wire rack. Serve warm or cold. (If they are not all eaten straightaway, store in an airtight container a couple of days.)

Leftovers for breakfast
crunchy muffin granola

This couldn't be easier and makes a great start to your day when eaten with milk or mixed with yogurt and fresh fruit for breakfast. Crumble **1 leftover muffin** into a bowl and then stir in **¼ cup rolled oats**, **1 tablespoon sunflower seeds**, **1 tablespoon flaxseed** (optional), **1 tablespoon shredded coconut** and **2 tablespoons warm honey**. Stir to combine, then put in a single layer on a baking sheet lined with parchment paper. Bake in an oven heated to 400°F 10 minutes. Stir in **2 tablespoons raisins**, **golden raisins**, **dried cranberries** or **dried cherries** and return to the oven 5 to 8 minutes until the granola is a deep golden brown. Leave to cool. This makes a generous adult portion or 2 smaller portions.

This makes a classic vanilla cake that can be transformed into any number of things, from a birthday cake to an impressive school cake-sale masterpiece. Alternatively, if you want to keep it simple, just fill with jam and whipped cream and dust the top with confectioners' sugar. This will certainly give you a thumbs up from your grandma!

Classic Vanilla Cake with Buttercream Frosting

MAKES one 8-inch cake
PREPARATION TIME 25 minutes
COOKING TIME 20 minutes

FOR THE CAKE
1 cup butter, soft, plus extra for greasing
2 cups less 2 tablespoons self-rising flour, sifted, plus 1 tablespoon extra for dusting
1 cup plus 2 tablespoons superfine sugar
1 teaspoon vanilla extract
4 eggs

FOR THE BUTTERCREAM FROSTING
1¾ cups plus 2 tablespoons unsalted butter, soft
3¼ cups confectioners' sugar, sifted
3 tablespoons milk
¼ teaspoon vanilla extract
food coloring (optional)

TO FINISH
4 to 5 tablespoons raspberry or strawberry jam
fresh strawberries or raspberries (optional)
your choice of cake decorations, sprinkles or candles (be as elaborate as you wish)

1 Heat the oven to 350°F. Grease two 8-inch round cake pans with butter and lightly dust with flour.

2 Using an electric mixer, in a large bowl, beat together the butter, sugar and vanilla extract a good few minutes until the mixture is wonderfully light and fluffy. Beat in the eggs one at a time, adding a spoonful of flour with each egg to prevent the batter curdling. Fold in the remaining flour with a large metal spoon until you have a soft, smooth cake batter.

3 Divide the batter between the prepared pans and level the tops with a spatula. Make a slight dip in the middle so the cakes bake flat. Bake the cakes about 20 minutes, until they spring back when pressed gently with a finger and are pale golden.

4 Leave the cakes to cool in the pans about 5 minutes, then remove from the pans and transfer to a wire rack to cool completely.

5 To make the buttercream frosting, using an electric mixer, beat together the butter, confectioners' sugar, milk and vanilla extract until the mixture is really light and creamy. Add a few drops of food coloring, if you like, and beat it in well.

6 Sandwich the cakes together with a layer of jam and a little buttercream frosting, then use the rest of the frosting to decorate the top and side, along with whatever else you choose to use. Serve with a flourish.

These little stunners don't take long to make and can act as lifesavers around the four-o'clock mark on Saturday or Sunday with a cup of tea or coffee. Any leftover cupcakes make a good treat during the week, because they store well for a couple of days in an airtight container. You can also make them with raspberries, small strawberries or blackberries instead of blueberries. Frozen berries are perfect to use when fresh ones are out of season.

OMG Blueberry and Lemon Cupcakes

MAKES 12 cupcakes
PREPARATION TIME 15 minutes
COOKING TIME 15 minutes

2¼ cups confectioners' sugar, sifted
⅔ cup all-purpose flour
½ cup very finely ground blanched almonds
½ cup shredded coconut
½ teaspoon baking powder
1 cup blueberries
½ cup unsalted butter, melted
finely grated zest of 1 large lemon
5 egg whites

1 Heat the oven to 350°F and line a 12-hole muffin pan with paper cupcake cases.

2 Mix together the confectioners' sugar, flour, grounds almonds, coconut, baking powder and blueberries. Add the butter, lemon zest and egg whites and mix until combined, then spoon into the muffin cases. Bake the cupcakes 15 minutes, or until they are lightly colored and just springy to the touch in the middle.

3 Leave to cool slightly in the pan before removing. Serve warm or cold. (The cupcakes will keep in an airtight container a few days and still remain really moist and yummy.)

This is one of those cake recipes that's perfect for a school cake sale or coffee morning, because it's very easy and doesn't require any fancy finishing. Nothing is wasted, either, as any leftover cake makes a perfect fruity base for a trifle or can even be made into Cake Pops (see page 220) your children are certain to love.

Lime and Orange Sheet Cake

MAKES 16 to 20 squares
PREPARATION TIME 15 minutes
COOKING TIME 25 minutes

1 cup butter, soft, plus extra for greasing
1 cup plus 2 tablespoons sugar
grated zest and juice of 2 limes
grated zest and juice of 1 large orange
½ teaspoon vanilla extract
3 eggs
1¾ cups plus 1 tablespoon self-raising
    flour
2 tablespoons milk

1 Heat the oven to 350°F. Grease an 8- x 12-inch cake pan with butter and line it with parchment paper.

2 Using an electric mixer, beat together the 1 cup plus 2 tablespoons of the sugar, the butter, lime and orange zests and vanilla extract until light and creamy. Beat in the eggs one at a time, adding a spoonful of the flour with each one to prevent the batter curdling. Mix in the remaining flour and the milk. Spoon the batter into the prepared pan and smooth the surface with a spatula. Bake the cake 25 minutes, or until it is golden and a skewer inserted into the middle comes out clean.

3 While the cake is baking, put the lime and orange juice in a small saucepan over medium heat. Bring to a boil, then boil to reduce to about ½ cup. Stir in the remaining sugar so it just starts to dissolve. As soon as the cake comes out of the oven, prick the top several times with a skewer or fork, then slowly spoon the lime and orange syrup all over the top, letting it soak into the cake.

4 Leave the cake to cool completely in the pan, then turn out and cut into pieces to serve.

Leftovers for yummy trifle
citrus trifles

This is a refreshing trifle that uses up any sheet cake that has become a little dry. Break the leftover cake into pieces and put them in the bottom of individual or one large serving bowl. Pour over just enough **orange juice**, **orange liqueur** or **limoncello** to moisten the cake. Top with a good portion of **sliced banana** and **cut-up orange**, **satsuma** or **mandarin segments**. Spoon over a thick layer of **bought** or **Foolproof Homemade Custard Sauce** (see page 114) and then a layer of **whipped cream**. Finally, swirl a little lemon curd into the cream for a ripple effect and scatter with **a handful of toasted slivered almond** and **a little freshly grated lemon zest**.

I have my grandma to thank for this recipe. She was always so organized, and she loved this cake because it could be made a day or so in advance, but would still be delicious and moist when it was needed. It's ideal for birthday parties, when making a cake on the day of the party would send you into meltdown.

Moist Chocolate Cake with Chocolate Fudge Frosting

MAKES one 8-inch cake
PREPARATION TIME 25 minutes
COOKING TIME 35 minutes

FOR THE CAKE
⅔ cup sunflower, peanut or canola oil, plus extra for greasing
1½ cups less 2 tablespoons self-rising flour, plus extra for dusting
4 tablespoons unsweetened cocoa powder
1 teaspoon baking soda
1 teaspoon baking powder
¾ cup sugar
2 tablespoons golden syrup or light corn syrup
2 eggs, lightly beaten
⅔ cup milk

FOR THE CHOCOLATE FUDGE FROSTING
1½ tablespoons unsweetened cocoa powder
3½ ounces dark chocolate, 70% cocoa solids, broken into small pieces
⅔ cup very soft butter
3 cups confectioners' sugar, sifted
½ teaspoon vanilla extract
a pinch salt

TO DECORATE
4 to 5 tablespoons raspberry or apricot jam
your choice of cake decorations, sprinkles or candles (be as elaborate as you wish)

1 Heat the oven to 315°F. Grease two 8-inch cake pans with oil and lightly dust with flour.

2 Sift the flour, cocoa powder, baking soda and baking powder into a large mixing bowl or food processor. Add the remaining cake ingredients and beat well to give a smooth, thick batter consistency. Divide the batter evenly between the prepared cake pans and bake the cakes 30 to 35 minutes until just firm to touch.

3 Leave the cakes to cool in the pans about 10 minutes, then them turn out onto a wire rack to cool completely. (If you are planning a party, the cake will keep moist a couple of days in an airtight container, either frosted or plain.)

4 To make the frosting, dissolve the cocoa powder in 3 tablespoons boiling water and leave to one side. Put the chocolate in a large, heatproof bowl. Rest the bowl over a pan of gently simmering water, so the bottom of the bowl does not touch the water. Stir occasionally until the chocolate melts. (Or melt the chocolate gently in a microwave.)

5 Using an electric mixer, in a large bowl, beat together the butter, confectioners' sugar, vanilla extract and salt until well combined, then add the melted chocolate and the cocoa powder. Beat for a few minutes until thick and creamy.

6 Sandwich the cakes together with the jam, then spread the chocolate fudge frosting over the top and side of the cake. Finish with any decorations and enjoy.

Freshly baked cookies still warm from the oven are virtually impossible to resist, so what can be better than having cookie dough in the freezer, ready to create virtually instant homemade cookies to enjoy with a glass of milk or a cup of coffee or tea. These are light and crisp on the edges, but slightly soft and chewy in the middle—otherwise known as perfect. For chocoholics, you can use chocolate chips instead of the fudge.

Fudge Freezer Cookies

MAKES 12 to 16 cookies
PREPARATION TIME 20 minutes
COOKING TIME 15 minutes

½ cup butter, soft
½ cup soft light brown sugar
1 tablespoon golden syrup or light corn syrup
1 teaspoon vanilla extract
1 egg yolk
1¼ cups plus 2 tablespoons all-purpose flour, plus extra for dusting
a pinch salt
½ cup small fudge chunks

1 Heat the oven to 400°F and line a cookie sheet with parchment paper.

2 Using an electric mixer, beat together the butter, sugar and golden syrup until light and creamy. Add the vanilla extract and egg yolk and beat together briefly before sifting in the flour and salt and mixing until you have a smooth dough. Finally, add the fudge chunks.

3 Using lightly floured hands to stop the dough sticking to you, roll the dough into 12 to16 balls. Put the balls on the prepared cookie sheet, making sure they are slightly apart. (If you don't want to bake all the cookies at once, put the remainder on a cookie sheet lined with plastic wrap that will sit flat in your freezer. Put it in the freezer and leave about 1 hour for the dough to become solid, then peel them away from the plastic wrap. Put the unbaked dough balls into a freezer bag or container to freeze up to 2 months.)

4 Bake the cookies 10 to 12 minutes until they are just beginning to become firm, but aren't too dark around the edges. (If you bake the cookies from frozen, allow about 15 minutes.)

5 Leave the cookies to cool on the cookie sheet a couple of minutes, then transfer to a wire rack to cool completely before serving. They will keep for a couple days in an airtight container.

So quick to make and almost as quick to disappear, these nutty, crumbly cookies are a real family favorite. They are also so easy to make that the kids can help you. Use chunky or smooth peanut butter, whichever you prefer or happen to have in the cupboard.

Peanut Butter and Jam Crumbly Cookies

MAKES 20 cookies
PREPARATION TIME 15 minutes
COOKING TIME 12 minutes

½ cup butter, soft, plus extra
   for greasing
⅓ cup sugar
5 tablespoons peanut butter
1 egg yolk
2 cups all-purpose flour
3½ tablespoons raspberry
   or strawberry jam

1 Heat the oven to 350°F and grease two cookie sheets with butter and line with parchment paper.

2 Using an electric mixer, in a large bowl, beat together the butter and sugar until light and creamy. Mix in the peanut butter and egg yolk until combined, then mix in the flour to give a soft dough.

3 Take a heaped teaspoonful of the dough and roll into a ball. Put it on one the prepared cookie sheets. Stick a thumb or finger into the middle of the dough ball to make an imprint deep enough to fill with about ½ teaspoon jam. Repeat using the remaining dough. Fill each imprint with jam, then bake the cookies 10 to 12 minutes until they are lightly colored.

4 Leave the cookies to cool on the cookie sheets a couple of minutes, then transfer to a wire rack to cool completely before serving. They will keep for a couple days in an airtight container.

When it's raining and you need something to do to keep the kids occupied, making and decorating these cookies is perfect. They are also great if you need a present for a holiday like Mother's Day or Father's Day or for a birthday, because they can be any shape, such a heart, and decorated accordingly, perhaps with more hearts … and a few kisses.

Get Creative Cut-Out Cookies

MAKES 30 to 40 cookies, depending on the size of cutters you use

PREPARATION TIME 15 minutes, plus 1 hour chilling

COOKING TIME 8 minutes

½ cup butter, soft
¾ cup sugar
1 egg
1 tablespoon golden syrup or light corn syrup
½ teaspoon vanilla extract
2¼ cups self-rising flour, plus extra for dusting
1 teaspoon baking powder
a pinch salt
any frostings or decorations you like

1 Using an electric mixer, in a large bowl, beat together the butter and sugar until light and creamy. Add the egg, golden syrup and vanilla extract, then mix in the flour, baking powder and salt to make a smooth dough. Divide the dough in half and wrap each half in plastic wrap. Put the dough in the refrigerator about 1 hour to become firm.

2 Heat the oven to 350°F and line one or two cookie sheets with parchment paper.

3 Dust the countertop and a rolling pin with flour, then roll out the dough to about ¼ inch thick. Using a cookie cutter, cut out whatever shapes you like and put them on the prepared cookie sheet(s). The cookies can sit relatively close to each other, because they don't spread much during baking. If you wanted to pierce a hole in the cookies to thread ribbon through after they bake, do this now, using the tip of a skewer. Reroll the trimmings to get as many cookies as possible.

4 Bake the cookies 8 minutes, or until they are golden brown. Leave them to cool on the cookie sheets.

5 Once cool, the biscuits can be left plain or decorated with any frostings or decorations you like. (Undecorated cookies are best stored in an airtight container.)

Lifesaver for after-school treats
cookie dough

If you don't want to bake loads of cookies all at once, it still makes sense to make this quantity of dough, because you'll then have a Lifesaver when you need to magic a few cookies if the children bring a friend home after school, or they just need something to amuse them. Wrap and label the dough. It will keep in the refrigerator up to 5 days, or in the freezer up to 3 months, then thaw, roll out and bake another day.

These work very well in my house as a bribe: "If you … get in the bath / get dressed / eat your lunch / do your homework … you can have one of my oat bars". They even work with my husband.

Oat Bars

MAKES 16 oat bars
PREPARATION TIME 10 minutes
COOKING TIME 40 minutes

½ cup butter, plus extra for greasing
1 cup unpacked soft light brown sugar
2 tablespoons golden syrup or light corn syrup
finely grated zest of 1 orange
2 cups rolled oats
1 cup dried fruit, such as raisins, golden raisins, cherries, cranberries, chopped apricots, mango, apple, figs, prunes and / or dates
4 tablespoons flaxseed (in an attempt to be healthy!; optional)

1 Heat the oven to 315°F. Grease an 8-inch square baking pan with butter and line with parchment paper.

2 Put the butter, sugar, golden syrup and orange zest in a small pan over low heat and gently melt together. Put the oats, dried fruit and flaxseed, if using, in a bowl, then pour in the melted butter and sugar mixture. Mix well to combine, then tip into the prepared pan. Press into the edges and flatten out with the back of a spoon.

3 Bake the oat bars 35 to 40 minutes until golden. Leave to cool in the pan a few minutes, then turn out, cut into pieces, leave to cool and serve.

Leftovers with fruit, yogurt and spice
apple oat-bar pots
The oat bars will keep up to 4 days in an airtight container. Rather than eating them as a snack, however, break them into small pieces and scatter over Greek yogurt and fresh fruit for breakfast or a dessert. If you want a big boost of energy to start your day, or a delicious sweet treat at the end of a meal, a single piece of these oat bars can go a long way. Another option is to make Apple Oat-Bar Pots as a great little dessert for the kids—or for you, because this recipe makes an individual portion. Break **1 oat bar** into small pieces and make alternate layers of **stewed apple** or **pear** or **applesauce**, **Greek yogurt** mixed with **a pinch ground cinnamon** and some the **oat bar pieces** in a glass or small dish. Finish with remaining **oat bar pieces**, then just sit back and enjoy.

A very naughty but nice treat, this is great for kids to make and give as gifts. You can pack them in little boxes or cellophane bags tied with a piece of ribbon. (But do make extra and keep a few back to share.) You'll get the best flavor if you use chocolate with more than 70 percent cocoa solids; avoid cheap imitations.

Chocolate Bombs

MAKES 28 bombs
PREPARATION TIME 20 minutes, plus
up to 1 hour chilling

6 ounces dark chocolate, 70% cocoa
solids, broken into small pieces
3 tablespoons butter
2 tablespoons golden syrup or light
corn syrup
5 ounces plain cookies
1 cup candied cherries

1 Put the chocolate, butter and golden syrup in a large heatproof bowl. Rest the bowl over a pan of gently simmering water, so the bottom of the bowl does not touch the water. Stir occasionally until the chocolate melts. (Alternatively, you can melt the ingredients in a microwave.)

2 Meanwhile, finely crush the cookies, either in a freezer bag by bashing with a rolling pin, or in a food processor.

3 Rinse the cherries in a strainer and pat dry, then put them on a cutting board. (Doing this takes away the stickiness.) Chop the cherries into small dice and add to the chocolate with four-fifths of the crushed cookies. Put the mixture in the refrigerator 30 minutes to 1 hour to become firm.

4 Take heaped teaspoonfuls at a time and roll into little balls or bombs. Roll the chocolate balls in the reserved cookie crumbs to coat evenly, and repeat until all the chocolate mixture has been used.

5 Once made, these will last for a couple of weeks in the refrigerator.

Weekends are all about having fun, and when it's cold and wet outside there's nothing my kids love more than chilling out and watching movies. To give them a real treat, we'll make this super popcorn to tuck into while they watch. It makes enough for you to enjoy, too, if you can spare a couple of hours to relax.

Sticky Toffee Popcorn

MAKES 4 to 8 portions
PREPARATION TIME 5 minutes, plus
   15 minutes cooling
COOKING TIME 5 minutes

1 tablespoon sunflower oil
¼ cup popping corn
3 tablespoons salted butter
¼ cup light muscovado sugar
2 tablespoons golden syrup or light
   corn syrup

1 Line a cookie sheet with parchment paper.

2 Heat the oil in a large saucepan over medium-high heat. Add the corn and swirl the pan around to coat the corn in the oil. Cover with a tight-fitting lid. Reduce the heat to low and leave the pan a few minutes until the popping stops, then remove the pan from the heat.

3 Meanwhile, put the butter, sugar and golden syrup in a separate pan over low heat until the butter melts. Increase the heat to medium and let the mixture bubble 2 minutes. Pour over the popcorn and stir to coat.

4 Spread the popcorn over the prepared cookie sheet and leave to cool about 15 minutes in a cool place (not the refrigerator) before serving.

Leftovers go savory
cheese and onion popcorn

If you have leftover **popping corn**, you can make savory popcorn. Put the popcorn in a large pan and pop following the method above. In a separate pan, over low heat, melt **3 tablespoons butter**. Stir in **1 teaspoon onion salt** and remove the pan from the heat. Pour the salted butter over the popcorn and scatter ⅓ **cup finely grated fresh Parmesan cheese** over. Put the lid on the pan and shake it vigorously to coat the popcorn in the flavored butter. Serve the popcorn warm or cold.

This Lebanese-inspired recipe can be served as an appetizer with warm pita bread, my favorite, or as part of a *maza* selection (the Lebanese equivalent of mezze), such as hummus, pickled chilies, stuffed grape leaves, bulgur wheat salad and olives.

Sautéed Chicken Livers with Pomegranate Molasses and Garlic

MAKES 2 adult portions
PREPARATION TIME 5 minutes
COOKING TIME 10 minutes

5 ounces chicken livers, thawed if frozen
1 tablespoon all-purpose flour
1 tablespoon olive oil
about 1 tablespoon butter
2 garlic cloves, finely chopped
2 tablespoons pomegranate molasses
1 tablespoon chopped flat-leaf parsley
    leaves
sea salt and freshly ground black pepper
toasted pita bread, to serve

1 Pick over the chicken livers and trim off any fatty bits and sinew. Pat them dry with paper towels. Season the flour lightly with salt and pepper, then toss with the livers so they are lightly coated in the flour.

2 Heat the oil in a skillet over high heat, add the livers and fry 5 to 6 minutes until the outsides are crisp, but the middles still a little pink (not raw).

3 Add the butter and, when bubbling, throw in the garlic and cook about 30 seconds. Add the pomegranate molasses and 1 tablespoon water. Turn the livers in the pan so they are coated in the bubbling, sticky sauce. Stir in the parsley and season lightly with salt and pepper.

4 Serve with toasted pita bread to mop up the sauce.

Leftovers for an aperitif

vodka, pomegranate and soda

The pomegranate molasses is ideal for making into a refreshing predinner drink. Pour **1 tablespoon pomegranate molasses** into a tall glass and add a **double or single shot of vodka (2 to 3 tablespoons)**. Add a few **ice cubes** and a **good squeeze of lime** and stir around. Top up with **soda water**. Garnish with **pomegranate seeds** and **mint leaves**.

Serve this alone as an appetizer or as part of a tapas selection—with olives, cured hams, Manchego cheese, marinated anchovies, tortilla or even any of your favorite antipasti. Just double up on the shrimp if you don't have chorizo, or even use a combination of shrimp and a few squid rings.

Spanish Shrimp with Sherry and Chorizo

MAKES 2 adult portions
PREPARATION TIME 10 minutes
COOKING TIME 15 minutes

2 tablespoons olive oil
4½ ounces raw chorizo sausage, cut into
 ½-inch-thick slices
2 garlic cloves, crushed
4 ounces raw shelled jumbo shrimp
⅓ cup dry sherry
½ can (15-oz.) crushed tomatoes
 or ¾ cup plus 2 tablespoons
 tomato puree
1 bottled or canned roasted red bell
 pepper, sliced into strips
1 teaspoon sherry vinegar
a pinch dried chili flakes
1 small handful flat-leaf parsley leaves,
 chopped
sea salt and freshly ground black pepper
crusty bread, to serve

1 Heat a skillet over medium heat. Add the oil and then add the chorizo. Cook the chorizo about 5 minutes until it is cooked through and releases lots of rich, red oil.

2 Add the garlic and shrimp and cook a couple minutes longer until the shrimp turn pink.

3 Add the sherry, tomatoes, red pepper, sherry vinegar and chili flakes. Season lightly with salt and pepper. Increase the heat and fry, stirring, 4 to 5 minutes.

4 Stir in the parsley and serve with some crusty bread.

Create this delightful combination of flavors to serve with warm focaccia or ciabatta bread as a sophisticated first course, and treat yourself to a chilled glass of your favorite white wine as the perfect partner.

Chili and Lemon Mozzarella with Pan-Fried Avocado

MAKES 2 adult portions
PREPARATION TIME 10 minutes, plus
  15 to 30 minutes marinating (optional)
COOKING TIME 5 minutes

4½ ounces buffalo mozzarella, torn
  into pieces
grated zest and juice of ½ small lemon
½ red chili, seeded and thinly sliced
2 tablespoons extra virgin olive oil, plus
  extra for frying and drizzling
1 ripe avocado
sea salt and freshly ground black pepper

1 Put the mozzarella in a shallow nonmetallic bowl. Mix together the lemon zest, juice, chili and olive oil. Season lightly with salt and pepper and pour over the mozzarella. Ideally, cover and leave to marinate in the refrigerator 15 to 30 minutes.

2 To prepare the avocado, cut it in half and remove the pit. Peel away the skin and cut the flesh into slices about ½ inch thick. Heat a good drizzle of olive oil in a skillet over medium heat, add the avocado and fry 1 to 2 minutes on each side until golden brown. Remove the avocado from the pan, drizzle with olive oil and season with salt and plenty freshly ground black pepper.

3 Serve hot, with the marinated mozzarella and a glass of chilled white wine.

Leftovers for snacks
mozzarella croque monsieur
If you have some marinated mozzarella and raw or pan-fried avocado left over, they are delicious made into a Italian-style Croque Monsieur. For a single portion, butter both sides of **2 pieces of bread**. Scatter small pieces of the **mozzarella** and **thinly sliced avocado** onto one piece of bread. Lay a piece of **cooked ham** or **prosciutto** on top, then cover with the remaining piece of bread. Press down firmly. Heat a good **drizzle of olive oil** in a skillet over medium heat, add the sandwich and fry 1 to 2 minutes on each side until the cheese is melting and the bread is toasted and golden. Serve hot.

Choose whatever flavored sausages you like for this substantial main course. I like using chunky French Toulouse sausages, or try venison or garlic-and-herb-flavored sausages. Dried Puy lentils work just as well, rather than the canned lentils I suggest here, but you'll need to cook them a little longer. Use a heaped ½ cup dried Puy lentils and add to the pan with ⅔ cup stock. Cook as in the recipe, but simmer 45 minutes, not 15 minutes.

Red Wine Sausages with Puy Lentils

MAKES 2 adult portions
PREPARATION TIME 10 minutes
COOKING TIME 45 minutes

1 tablespoon olive oil
6 chunky link sausages
1 small red onion, finely sliced
½ large or 1 small red bell pepper,
    seeded and thinly sliced
1 cup plus 2 tablespoons red wine
1 or 2 oregano, thyme or rosemary
    sprigs (optional)
1¼ cups canned Puy lentils, drained
½ can (15-oz.) crushed tomatoes
3½ ounces baby or young spinach leaves
sea salt and freshly ground black pepper

1 Heat the oil in a deep skillet over medium heat, add the sausages and fry 10 to 15 minutes until they are evenly brown. Remove them from the pan and leave to one side.

2 Add the onion and red pepper to the pan and fry 5 to 8 minutes until they are soft and the onion is becoming golden. Return the sausages to the pan. Add the red wine and the herb sprigs, if using. Bring to a boil and boil a couple of minutes. Stir in the lentils and tomatoes. Bring to a boil, then reduce the heat, cover with a lid and leave to simmer gently 15 minutes.

3 Uncover, stir in the spinach until it wilts and is heated through, then season lightly with salt and pepper.

4 Spoon the lentils into two bowls or deep plates, top with the sausages and spoon any cooking liquid over to serve.

This Middle Eastern-inspired dish features spicy lamb complemented by a fresh salad with a lemony tang. Try to cook the lamb so it is still slightly pink in the middle for the best flavor. Sumac is a tart, acidic berry that's ground to a reddish-colored powder and used widely in Middle Eastern cooking. It's usually found in the dried spice section of some supermarkets, Middle Eastern food stores and gourmet delis, so the next time you see some, grab a jar. It adds a delicious tangy, lemony flavor to meat, fish, salads, hummus, rice dishes and much more. If you don't have any, replace it with a good squeeze of lemon juice in this recipe.

Spiced Lamb and Chickpeas with Sumac, Parsley and Tomato Salad

MAKES 2 adult portions
PREPARATION TIME 15 minutes
COOKING TIME 10 minutes

FOR THE SPICED LAMB
2 lamb leg steaks (bone in, if possible, for a better flavor)
2 tablespoons olive oil
1 teaspoon ground cumin
½ teaspoon paprika
¼ teaspoon cayenne pepper
½ can (15-oz.) chickpeas, drained
1 cup ripe kalamata olives, halved and pitted
¼ cup white wine or chicken stock
sea salt and freshly ground black pepper

FOR THE SUMAC, PARSLEY AND TOMATO SALAD
3 ripe tomatoes, cut into wedges
½ red onion, thinly sliced
1 small handful flat-leaf parsley leaves, roughly chopped
1 teaspoon sumac
1 tablespoon extra virgin olive oil

TO SERVE
3 tablespoons Greek yogurt mixed with 1 tablespoon chopped mint leaves
broiled or grilled flatbread or pita bread (optional)

1 Put the lamb in a flat dish and rub in 1 tablespoon of the olive oil, along with the cumin, paprika and cayenne. Leave to one side while you prepare the salad.

2 Meanwhile, toss together the salad ingredients and season with salt and pepper, then set aside.

3 Heat the remaining olive oil in a skillet over medium heat, add the lamb steaks and fry 2 to 3 minutes on each side until light brown and still slightly soft to the touch, which will give you medium lamb. Cook a shorter or longer time depending on how you like your meat cooked. Remove the lamb steaks from the pan and leave to rest.

4 Add the chickpeas and olives to the pan and toss around a couple of minutes to heat through. Add the wine, bring to a boil and boil 30 seconds. Season lightly with salt and pepper, then pour in any of the lamb resting juices.

5 Put the lamb steaks, chickpeas and salad on plates and serve with the minty Greek yogurt and flatbreads or pita bread, if you like.

Chimichurri is a tangy South American sauce for steak that makes this recipe into a delicious Saturday night treat, especially if you serve the steaks with chunky French fries. A ¾-inch-thick steak at room temperature takes about 5 minutes to cook to medium-rare if the pan is really hot before you put it in. Any leftover sauce keeps a few days in the refrigerator to serve with broiled, roasted or fried chicken or fish. You can also use it as a marinade or toss it with cooked vegetables.

Pan-Fried Chimichurri Steak

MAKES 2 adult portions
PREPARATION TIME 10 minutes
COOKING TIME 5 minutes

FOR THE STEAKS
a drizzle oil
2 good-quality steaks, whichever cut you prefer, such as rib-eye, sirloin or filet mignon, left at room temperature about 30 minutes before cooking
sea salt and freshly ground black pepper

FOR THE CHIMICHURRI SAUCE
1 tablespoon chopped flat-leaf parsley leaves
1 teaspoon fresh oregano leaves
2 garlic cloves, roughly chopped
3 tablespoons extra virgin olive oil
1 tablespoon red wine vinegar
a pinch dried chili flakes

TO SERVE
½ recipe quantity Oven-Baked French Fries (see below)
roasted vine tomatoes (optional)

1 To make the chimichurri sauce, put the parsley, oregano and garlic in a small food processor or blender and whiz until finely chopped, then stir in the olive oil, red wine vinegar and chili flakes. Season with salt and pepper and leave to one side until ready to serve.

2 To cook the steaks, put a griddle or large skillet over high heat and leave it to become super-hot, then add a trickle of oil. If the steaks are wet, pat them dry with paper towels, then season generously with salt and pepper. As soon as the oil is smoking hot, add the steaks to the pan and cook about 1½ minutes, flip them over and cook a minute or so longer, then flip over every minute until the steaks are cooked to your liking. If there is a thick piece of fat around the edge of the steaks, use a pair of tongs to hold the steak vertically in the pan to brown the fat.

3 Remove the steaks from the pan and leave to rest in a warm place at least 5 minutes. Serve the steaks with any resting juices poured over, and spoon some chimichurri sauce on top. Serve with oven-baked French fries and roasted vine tomatoes, if you like.

How to make
oven-baked French fries or wedges
Put a large, nonstick baking sheet or roasting pan in the oven and heat until the oven temperature reaches 400°F. Cut **1 pound 10 ounces Idaho potatoes** or **sweet potatoes** into French fry shapes or slim wedges, peeled or not, as you prefer. Toss the potatoes in **3 tablespoons olive oil** and transfer to the hot pan. Return the pan to the oven and bake the potatoes 25 to 45 minutes (depending on the thickness of the potatoes), turning them every 10 minutes or so until they are cooked through and golden brown. Once baked, season with **salt** to taste. For added flavor, toss **2 teaspoons dried spices** with the potatoes before baking. My favorites are **paprika**, **mild chili powder**, **garam masala**, **sumac** and **Cajun** or **Creole** seasoning. Choose flavors that complement the main dish. This makes enough for 4 adult portions.

For an Asian twist on French *moules-frîtes*, this makes a fabulous main-course served with Oven-Baked French Fries (see page 148), seasoned with sea salt and finely grated lime zest.

Fragrant Coconut and Chili Mussels

MAKES 2 adult portions
PREPARATION TIME 15 minutes
COOKING TIME 15 minutes

2¼ pounds live mussels
1 tablespoon sunflower oil
2 shallots, finely chopped
1 red chili, seeded and finely sliced
¾-inch piece gingerroot, peeled and
   finely chopped
1 lemongrass stalk, outer layer removed
   and the rest finely chopped
⅔ cup white wine
⅔ cup coconut cream
2 teaspoons Thai fish sauce
finely grated zest and juice of 1 lime
1 small handful cilantro leaves, chopped

TO SERVE
½ recipe quantity Oven-Baked Fench
   Fries (see page 148)
sea salt

1 Scrub the mussels thoroughly with a stiff brush under cold running water to remove all traces of grit, then remove any barnacles or other debris attached to the shells and pull off and discard any beards. Rinse again and discard any mussels that stay open.

2 Heat the oil in a wok or large saucepan over medium heat, add the shallots, chili, ginger and lemongrass and fry 4 to 5 minutes until the shallots are soft but not colored. Increase the heat to high, stir in the wine and bring to a boil. Carefully toss in the mussels and stir around, then cover the pan with a lid or, if you don't have one big enough, cover with a cookie sheet. Simmer 5 to 6 minutes until the mussels open, shaking the pan a couple of times. Discard any that remain closed or will not open easily.

3 Stir the coconut cream, fish sauce and lime juice into the pan and cook 1 minute, stirring. Using a slotted spoon, lift the mussels out of the pan into bowls. Return the wok or pan to the heat and boil a couple minutes to reduce the sauce until it thickens slightly. Stir in the cilantro, then pour over the mussels.

4 Sprinkle with the grated lime zest and serve with fries seasoned lightly with sea salt.

It's Saturday night, the kids are all fast asleep (fingers crossed) and I'm reliably informed that mushrooms have considerable aphrodisiac qualities. I'll say no more ...

Your Lucky Night Gnocchi

MAKES 2 adult portions
PREPARATION TIME 10 minutes, plus
   20 minutes soaking
COOKING TIME 15 minutes

½ ounce dried porcini, morel or mixed
   wild mushrooms
12 ounces to 1 pound 2 ounces bought
   gnocchi (depending on how hungry
   you are)
1 tablespoon olive oil
3 tablespoons butter
3½ cups thinly sliced cremini
   mushrooms
2 garlic cloves, crushed
½ cup half-fat sour cream
¼ cup freshly grated Parmesan cheese
a squeeze lemon juice
1 small handful flat-leaf parsley leaves,
   chopped
sea salt and freshly ground black pepper

1 Cover the dried mushrooms with hot water and leave to soak 15 to 20 minutes.

2 Bring a pan of salted water to a boil, add the gnocchi and return to a boil. Boil 2 minutes, or according to the package directions, then drain well.

3 Meanwhile, heat a large skillet over medium heat, add the olive oil and butter and heat until the butter is bubbling. Add the cremini mushrooms and cook 5 to 6 minutes until soft.

4 Strain the dried mushrooms, reserving the soaking liquid, and squeeze out any excess water. Add the mushrooms to the skillet with the garlic and cook a couple minutes. Stir in the sour cream, about ½ cup of the mushroom soaking liquid, the Parmesan, lemon juice and parsley. Season lightly with salt and pepper and cook until hot but not quite boiling, or the sour cream might curdle.

5 Toss in the gnocchi and cook in the pan for a minute or so to soak up the flavors. Serve the gnocchi with a little extra mushroom soaking liquid spooned over the top.

Unless I'm entertaining, desserts tend to be the last thing on my mind. If you're like me, all you'll want to do is have a nice main course, then fall asleep halfway through a movie. But this dessert is so simple to make and so more-ish, it might even give you the impetus to stay awake through the other half of that movie. Or, try this with thinly sliced pears, peaches, plums, apricots or apple instead of the figs.

Fig Tartlets with Orange Mascarpone

MAKES 2 adult portions
PREPARATION TIME 15 minutes
COOKING TIME 15 minutes

FOR THE ORANGE MASCARPONE
½ cup mascarpone
finely grated zest of ½ small orange, plus a little extra for sprinkling
½ teaspoon vanilla extract
2 tablespoons confectioners' sugar, sifted
1 tablespoon milk

FOR THE FIG TARTLETS
butter, for greasing
⅓ sheet rolled puff pastry dough, thawed if frozen
2 tablespoons apricot jam
2 or 3 ripe figs, very thinly sliced
1 egg yolk
1 tablespoon milk
confectioners' sugar, for dusting

1 Beat together all the orange mascarpone ingredients until you have a smooth cream. (You can prepare the mascarpone up to 24 hours in advance and keep it in the refrigerator.)

2 Heat the oven to 400°F and lightly grease a large cookie sheet with butter.

3 Using a sharp knife, cut the pastry dough into 2 circles or heart shapes about 4 inches in diameter. Put them onto the prepared cookie sheet and score a small border of about ½ inch around the edge of each one and prick the middle a couple of times with a fork.

4 Spread 1 tablespoon of the apricot jam in the middle of each piece of dough, then arrange the figs in an overlapping circle on top. (The tartlets can be assembled several hours ahead of baking and kept covered with plastic wrap in the refrigerator at this stage.) Mix together the egg yolk and milk to make an egg wash. Brush the top of the figs and the dough edges with the egg wash, then dust each one fairly generously with confectioners' sugar. Bake the tartlets 15 minutes, or until the pastry is puffed up and golden brown around the edges.

5 Dust the tartlets with more confectioners' sugar and serve hot, warm or cool with a good spoonful of the orange mascarpone, sprinkled with a little extra zest.

Leftovers for lunch
cheesy tomato pastries

Cut any remaining **puff pastry dough** into 2 to 4 rectangles and spread **a little Dijon mustard** or **ketchup** onto one half of each surface. Scatter with a melting cheese, such as **grated Edam, Gouda, Gruyère, Swiss** or **Jarlsberg**, then add **1 to 2 tomato slices**. Mix together **1 egg yolk** and **1 tablespoon milk** to make an egg wash. Brush the edges of the dough with the egg wash and fold over the other half of dough, sealing the edges by pressing with the back of a fork. Put the pastries on a greased cookie sheet, brush the top with a little more egg wash and scatter with more cheese. Bake in an oven heated to 425°F 10 to 12 minutes. Leave the pastries to cool a few minutes before serving.

I love desserts that are simple, yet look impressive—and here is one that ticks all the boxes. You can use other crackers or cookies, if you like. Gingernut cookies with lemon yogurt makes a good combination, for example.

Easy-Yet-Impressive Raspberry Cheesecake Pots

MAKES 2 adult portions
PREPARATION TIME 10 minutes, plus at least
   30 minutes chilling

3 graham crackers
1 tablespoon butter, melted
½ cup cream cheese
5 tablespoons raspberry yogurt
2 tablespoons confectioners' sugar
finely grated zest of ½ lemon, plus
   1 teaspoons grated lemon zest,
   to decorate
⅔ cup raspberries
2 tablespoons bought raspberry
   coulis or sauce

1 Put the graham crackers in a food processor and blitz until they become fine crumbs. Alternatively, you can put the crackers in a sandwich bag and crush with a rolling pin. Mix the cracker crumbs with the melted butter and then press the crumbs into the bottom of two glasses or dishes.

2 Mix together the cream cheese, yogurt, confectioners' sugar and lemon zest until smooth. You might find a balloon whisk best for this. Mix the raspberries with the coulis or sauce. Make alternate layers of the raspberries and the cheesecake mixture on top of the crumb crusts.

3 Put the glasses in the refrigerator to chill at least 30 minutes. (The finished cheesecake pots can be made several hours ahead and kept in the refrigerator.) Serve decorated with the 1 teaspoon grated lemon zest.

Leftovers for liqueur treats
boozy chocolate truffles

If you have opened a package of graham crackers especially for the cheesecake pots, the leftovers are ideal to make into these delicious chocolate truffles. Keep them simple for the kids or add a liqueur for an after-dinner treat for the adults. Finely crush **8 graham crackers**. Melt together **2½ ounces dark chocolate (70% cocoa solids), 1 tablespoon golden syrup** or **light corn syrup, 1 tablespoon unsweetened cocoa powder** and **3 tablespoons butter.** Add about **2 tablespoons of your favorite liqueur**, such as brandy, Scotch, orange liqueur, rum, coconut liqueur or whatever you like. Mix in the cracker crumbs and shape into balls. Roll in a little **unsweetened cocoa powder**, then chill to set. These will keep about 2 weeks in an airtight container in the refrigerator.

CLING ONTO YOUR SOCIAL LIFE

You need to let your hair down now and again ...

My life as a mom means I get to spend less quality time with my friends. For one, flopping on the sofa (once you've got everyone fed, washed and into bed, then tidied up) on a Saturday night with a large glass of wine is more appealing than throwing a dinner party. In the back of your mind, however, you know you should cling onto your social life just for your own sanity, and a good adult gossip is a wonderful antidote to the crazy conversations you've been having all week with your children.

So this chapter is all about getting people over to your place for a bite to eat, a chat and a few drinks, but taking into account cooking for four or six or even eight—depending on the size of your dining table—takes effort. I've thought about everything to help make your gathering as stress-free as possible by using all the tricks I know. All the recipes are easy to shop for, simple to prepare and a doddle to cook, leaving you time to enjoy being with your friends and reminiscing about your carefree old life. But make sure you don't talk about children—the subject is totally banned at all dinner parties.

As a flavorful alternative to a classic peach Bellini, this sweet mango and fragrant lychee cocktail makes a great combination, but you don't have to stop here. Try other types of soft fruit, such as raspberries or even a mixture of berries—in fact, go mad! Become famous for your fruity combos among your friends, open a Bellini bar, turn it into a franchise and become rich beyond your wildest dreams …

Mango and Lychee Bellini

MAKES 8 glasses
PREPARATION TIME 10 minutes

1 large ripe mango, pitted, peeled and
   roughly chopped
8 canned lychees, plus 2 tablespoons
   of the lychee juice or syrup
1 bottle of chilled prosecco, cava
   or champagne

1 Put the mango and lychees in a blender with the juice and blend until you have a really smooth puree. (The puree can be made a couple of days in advance and kept in the refrigerator.)

2 Divide the puree into 8 champagne flutes, then pour in a little sparkling wine. Stir to mix, then slowly top up the glasses with the remaining sparkling wine.

How to make
berry puree

If you prefer your Bellini with berries, here's how to make the puree. Blend **1½ cups fresh or frozen berries** to a smooth puree. Have a taste and if they are too sharp, add **a little sifted confectioners' sugar** until they are as sweet as like them. Press the puree through a strainer, leaving any seeds behind. To make berry Bellinis, half fill champagne flutes with **chilled sparkling wine** or **champagne**, then stir in **1 tablespoon of the puree** and **1 tablespoon berry liqueur**, such as crème de cassis (black currant), Chambord (raspberry), crème du muré (blackberry) or kirsch (cherry). Stir to mix and slowly top up with more sparkling wine. Any leftover puree can be kept in the refrigerator a few days or stored in the freezer up to 3 months.

Leftovers for an ice cream sauce
mango and lychee puree

It's well worth making extra puree so you have lots more than you need. It's delicious **poured onto ice cream** to make a sundae, **stirred into whipped cream** for desserts or **mixed into yogurt**. I really like to **freeze it in ice-cube trays** so I can quickly thaw one and enjoy a Mango and Lychee Bellini any time I'm in the mood.

The traditional Moscow Mule is a combination of vodka, ginger beer and lime—so it has quite a kick. I started with the basic recipe and played around with it a bit to create my own version, with mint and Angostura bitters. If vodka is not your spirit of choice, try one of the alternatives I've suggested, or try out some new ideas of your own— recipe testing cocktails doesn't count toward your weekly alcohol consumption (well, that's my rule). If you can't find ginger beer (not ginger ale) look for it in a Caribbean food store.

Traveling Mules

MAKES 2 glasses
PREPARATION TIME 5 minutes

FOR MOSCOW MULE
ice cubes
5 tablespoons vodka
2 tablespoons lime juice
1 cup plus 2 tablespoons chilled ginger beer
Angostura bitters
mint sprigs and thin gingerroot slices, to serve

FOR TRAVELING MULES
for variety, swap the vodka for a different spirit:
FOR JAMAICAN MULES
dark, white or spiced rum
FOR MEXICAN MULES
tequila
FOR ENGLISH MULES
gin

1 Half fill two tall glasses with ice cubes. Divide the vodka and lime juice between the glasses and stir.

2 Top up with ginger beer, add a couple of shakes of Angostura bitters to each glass and stir again.

3 Decorate with mint sprigs and thin slices of ginger to serve.

A perfect drink to serve when it's chilly, you can even make this child or driver friendly by leaving out the calvados. Another option is to make it with plain brandy, and vanilla-flavored vodka is also nice.

Hot Apple Spice Punch

MAKES 8 large glasses
PREPARATION TIME 15 minutes

6½ cups apple juice
1 cup plus 2 tablespoons calvados
  (applejack)
4 cinnamon sticks
1 teaspoon whole cloves
1 teaspoon allspice berries
¼ cup demerara sugar
peeled strips of zest from
  2 oranges

1 Put all the ingredients in a saucepan over medium-low heat. Making sure it doesn't boil, stir until the sugar dissolves.

2 Continue simmering about 10 minutes to let the flavors infuse. Serve hot in heatproof glasses or cups.

Leftovers for a Gallic supper
pork chops with apple-cream sauce

Once you've bought a bottle of **calvados** you'll find many uses for it. Stir it into **whipped cream** to serve with **apple or pear tarts**, **crumbles**, **pies** or **cakes**, or use it to make this delicious pork dish. Cook **2 pork chops** in a skillet over medium-low heat 7 to 8 minutes on each side until cooked through, then leave to rest. Increase the heat to high, add **½ peeled, cored and finely diced apple** and **⅓ cup calvados** and bubble about 30 seconds, then add **½ cup less 2 tablespoon heavy cream** and **1 tablespoon chopped sage**. Bring to a boil and boil 30 seconds, season lightly with **sea salt** and **freshly ground black pepper** and serve poured over the pork chops.

I love a martini to kick-start an evening and to welcome my friends to a fun night ahead. Apple, Elderflower and Cassis has turned into my signature Madhouse Martini—mainly due to the fact I usually have all the ingredients and can shake one together in no time at all. Lemongrass, Ginger and Mint is tangy and aromatic, and ideal to serve before Asian cuisine. And to end an evening on a high, the Espresso Martini is an absolute must for coffee lovers.

Madhouse Martinis

EACH ONE MAKES 2 glasses
PREPARATION TIME 10 minutes each

APPLE, ELDERFLOWER AND CASSIS MARTINI

ice cubes
5 tablespoons gin
5 tablespoons apple juice
2 tablespoons elderflower cordial
1 tablespoon crème de cassis
thin apple slices, to serve

1 Half fill a cocktail shaker with ice, then add the gin, apple juice, elderflower cordial and crème de cassis. Shake a good 30 seconds.

2 Pour into two martini glasses and serve with thin apple slices.

LEMONGRASS, GINGER AND MINT MARTINI

1 stalk lemongrass, outer layer removed and the rest roughly chopped
about 15 mint leaves, plus extra to garnish
1½ tablespoons roughly chopped preserved ginger
ice cubes
4 tablespoons preserved ginger syrup
½ cup vodka
juice of ½ lime

1 Put the lemongrass, mint leaves and preserved ginger in a mortar and pestle, mini food processor or even a strong sandwich bag and bash or whiz to a rough paste. (This can be done well ahead of time and kept in the refrigerator until needed.) Transfer to a cocktail shaker half filled with ice, then add the ginger syrup, vodka and lime juice. Shake a good 30 seconds.

2 Strain through a fine strainer or tea strainer into two martini glasses and serve with extra mint leaves.

ESPRESSO MARTINI

ice cubes
⅓ cup freshly made espresso
⅓ cup vodka
⅓ cup Kahlúa or Tia Maria coffee liqueur
2 tablespoons crème de cacao chocolate liqueur (optional)
a few whole coffee beans, to serve

1 Half fill a cocktail shaker with ice, then add the hot espresso, vodka, coffee liqueur and crème de cacao, if using. Shake a good 30 seconds.

2 Pour into two martini glasses, add a couple of coffee beans and serve.

You can make these as spicy as you like—the spicier the better in my house so the kids won't eat them all before my guests arrive—but, whatever you do, make plenty, as they are very more-ish.

Thai Sausage and Peanut Rolls

MAKES about 30 rolls
PREPARATION TIME 25 minutes
COOKING TIME 25 minutes

oil, for greasing
⅓ cup unsalted, skinned peanuts
9 ounces sausagemeat
1 to 2 tablespoons Thai red curry paste (depending on how much spice you want)
1 large handful cilantro leaves, roughly chopped
13 ounces rolled puff pastry dough, thawed if frozen
all-purpose flour, for dusting
1 egg yolk
1 tablespoon milk

TO SERVE
chili dipping sauce
1 lime, cut into wedges

1 Heat the oven to 375°F and grease a cookie sheet.

2 Put the peanuts in a food processor and whiz until finely chopped. Remove one-third from the bowl and set aside. Add the sausagemeat, Thai red curry paste and cilantro to the food processor bowl and whiz again to combine.

3 Lay the pastry dough flat on a lightly floured countertop and cut into two long strips. Mix together the egg yolk and milk to make an egg wash, then brush the edges of the dough with a little of the egg wash. Using wet hands to stop the sausagemeat sticking to you, divide it in half and shape each piece into a long, thin sausage, the same length as the dough. Put one piece of sausagemeat on top of each dough strip, then fold over the dough to seal in the sausagemeat. Roll the whole thing over so the sealed edge is underneath. (The sausage rolls can now be kept in the refrigerator 24 hours, lightly covered with plastic wrap, or they can even be frozen up to 3 months and thawed before cooking.)

4 Using a sharp knife, cut into bite-size sausage rolls, discarding the dough ends, and score a couple of slits in the top of each one. Brush with the remaining egg wash and scatter the reserved peanuts over. Carefully lift onto the prepared cookie sheet and bake 20 to 25 minutes until the sausagemeat is cooked through and the pastry is golden.

5 Serve warm with chili dipping sauce and lime wedges. (If you make these ahead of time, they can be reheated in a low oven.)

If you can find packages of unsweetened crepes, they are ideal to use for this recipe. If you can't get hold of crepes, however, wheat tortillas make a good alternative, and a can of crabmeat is a good substitute for the smoked salmon.

Smoked Salmon, Caper and Dill Crepe Rolls

MAKES about 20 mini rolls
PREPARATION TIME 20 minutes

¾ cup plus 2 tablespoons cream cheese
1½ tablespoons chopped dill
1 tablespoon capers, rinsed and finely chopped
grated zest and juice of ½ lemon
4 bought crepes or homemade Foolproof Crepes (see page 86)
5 ounces thinly sliced smoked salmon
sea salt and freshly ground black pepper

1 Mix together the cream cheese, dill, capers, lemon zest and juice until creamy, then season lightly with salt and pepper.

2 Spread the mixture over the crepes, then top with the smoked salmon. Roll up each crepe tightly to form a long roll. (You can now wrap the rolls in plastic wrap and keep in the refrigerator until needed. This can be done a day ahead.)

3 Trim away the ends and cut into neat 1-inch slices. If any happen to unroll, use toothpicks to secure them. Serve straightaway or keep covered in the refrigerator until ready to serve.

Leftovers for more-ish crepes

savory baked crepes

Any leftover crepes make a great meal for the kids. Fill them with **baked beans**, **spaghetti sauce** or **ratatouille**. Roll them up and put them in a baking dish, scatter with **grated cheese** and bake in an oven heated to 400°F about 10 minutes until golden and bubbling.

Of course, there's nothing to stop you using Beluga caviar instead of the cheaper version if you like! Using bought blinis makes the recipe very quick and easy, but if you have the time it's satisfying to make your own, so have a go with my recipe below.

Crab and Avocado Blinis

MAKES 12 to 16 blinis
PREPARATION TIME 15 minutes
COOKING TIME 10 minutes if cooking your
   own blinis

12 to 16 bought mini or cocktail blinis
   or ½ recipe quantity Cocktail Blinis
   (below)
1 ripe avocado, halved and pitted
juice of ½ lemon
1 tablespoon olive oil
a splash hot-pepper sauce
3½ ounces fresh white crabmeat
2 to 3 tablespoons mayonnaise
sea salt and freshly ground black pepper

TO SERVE
1 to 2 teaspoons lumpfish caviar
   (optional)
a few chives

1 If you are using bought blinis, warm them according to the package directions. This makes them lighter in texture than if you use them straight from the package. If you are making your own, follow the directions below.

2 Scoop the flesh out of the avocado and mash with the back of a fork, then mix in a good squeeze of lemon juice, the oil and hot-pepper sauce and season lightly with salt and pepper.

3 In a separate bowl, mix together the crabmeat, mayonnaise and a squeeze of lemon juice. Season with salt and pepper, if needed. Spoon the avocado mixture on top of the blinis, then top with some crab. Top each one with lumpfish caviar, if you like, and a small piece of chive.

4 Cover and keep in the refrigerator several hours until you are ready to serve.

How to make
cocktail blinis

To make about 24 blinis, beat **⅔ cup buckwheat flour** with **1 teaspoon baking powder**, **1 lightly beaten egg**, **1½ cup milk** and **a pinch salt**. Heat **a drop of oil** in a skillet over medium heat until hot, then drop in spoonfuls of the batter and fry a minute or so on each side until pale golden brown. Once cooked and cooled, they can be frozen up to 3 months.

These are so easy to put together and make a colorful plate of nibbles to entice your guests. For a slightly sweeter version, spread the pastry dough with a spoonful of cranberry sauce and chunks of Brie.

Cherry Tomato and Feta Pastry Squares

MAKES about 30 squares
PREPARATION TIME 15 minutes
COOKING TIME 15 minutes

7 ounces rolled puff pastry dough,
   thawed if frozen
olive oil, for brushing
1 cup crumbled feta cheese
15 cherry tomatoes, halved
15 ripe olives, pitted and halved
sea salt and freshly ground black pepper

1 Heat the oven to 400°F and line a cookie sheet with parchment paper.

2 Cut the pastry dough into 1-inch squares and put on the prepared cookie sheet. Prick each square a few times with a fork. Brush the dough with olive oil, then top with crumbled feta. Put a tomato half and ripe olive on each one, then season lightly with salt and pepper. (They can be prepared up to this stage the day before required and kept in the refrigerator, loosely covered with plastic wrap.)

3 Bake the dough squares 15 minutes, or until the pastry is golden brown. Serve warm or at room temperature.

Leftovers for mini pies
savory or sweet pastry puffs

Get the kids involved in using up the leftover pastry dough. Use mini cutters to cut out dough shapes and put them on a greased cookie sheet lined with parchment paper. Mix **1 egg yolk** with **1 tablespoon milk** to make an egg wash and brush over the surface of the dough. For a savory version, top each one with **finely grated fresh Parmesan** or **Gruyère cheese** and **poppy seeds** or **sesame seeds**. For sweet pastry puffs, generously sprinkle **sugar** over or use a **flavored sugar**, such as vanilla sugar or cinnamon sugar. Bake in an oven heated to 400°F 5 to 8 minutes until puffed up and golden brown, then serve.

You can whiz together these delicious dips in minutes to serve with tortilla chips, potato chips, breadsticks, pita bread, carrot, cucumber, celery, bell peppers, radishes—actually, whatever you like. They can all be made a day in advance and stored in the refrigerator, but take them out 30 minutes before serving to get the most out of their flavors.

Quick Dips

EACH ONE MAKES 4 to 6 adult portions
PREPARATION TIME 5 minutes each

ARTICHOKE, ARUGULA AND PARMESAN DIP

10 ounces bottled artichokes in oil
1¾ ounces arugula leaves
½ cup freshly grated Parmesan cheese
juice of ½ lemon
2 tablespoons extra virgin olive oil
sea salt and freshly ground black pepper

1 Drain half of the oil from the artichokes and put the remaining oil with the artichokes in a food processor along with the arugula leaves, Parmesan, lemon juice and extra virgin olive oil. Season lightly with salt and pepper and whiz to a paste. Spoon the dip into a serving bowl and chill in the refrigerator.

2 When ready to serve, give the dip a little stir first.

CARAMELIZED ONION AND DOLCELATTE DIP

5 ounces dolcelatte cheese
⅔ cup half-fat sour cream
1 tablespoon lemon juice
freshly ground black pepper
sea salt (optional)
3 tablespoons bottled caramelized
   onions

1 Whiz together the dolcelatte, sour cream, lemon juice and plenty of freshly ground black pepper in a food processor until smooth. You shouldn't need to add salt, because the cheese is naturally salty, but add some if you think the dip needs it.

2 Spoon the dip into a serving bowl and spoon the onions on top. Use the handle of a teaspoon to lightly swirl them into the top of the creamy cheese, then serve.

CREAMY MUSTARD AND SCALLION DIP

¾ cup plus 2 tablespoons half-fat
   sour cream
1 tablespoon Dijon mustard
2 teaspoons honey
4 scallions, very finely chopped
sea salt

1 Simply mix everything together, spoon into a dish and serve.

BEET AND SOUR CREAM DIP

1¼ cups chopped cooked beets (not in vinegar)
5 tablespoons sour cream
⅔ cup mayonnaise
1 tablespoon snipped chives
sea salt and freshly ground black pepper

1 Whiz the beets, sour cream, mayonnaise, salt and pepper in a food processor until smooth and a fabulous pink color.

2 Spoon into a serving bowl and serve sprinkled with the chives.

SPICY WHITE BEAN AND RED PEPPER DIP

½ can (15-oz.) canned white beans, such as navy or butter beans, drained
2 bottled or canned roasted red bell peppers
½ cup finely ground blanched almonds
2 garlic cloves, crushed
juice of ½ lemon
½ teaspoon dried chili flakes, plus extra for sprinkling
3 tablespoons extra virgin olive oil, plus extra for drizzling
sea salt and freshly ground black pepper

1 Put all the ingredients in a food processor and whiz until smooth. Have a taste and add any extra seasoning, chili flakes, lemon juice or olive oil, depending on your personal preference.

2 Spoon into a serving bowl, add a drizzle of olive oil and a sprinkling of chili flakes, and serve.

PEA, GOAT CHEESE AND MINT DIP

2 cups frozen peas, thawed
5 ounces soft goat cheese
1 large handful mint leaves, plus extra for sprinkling
1 garlic clove, crushed
finely grated zest of 1 lemon
juice of ½ lemon, plus extra for sprinkling
2 tablespoons extra virgin olive oil
sea salt and freshly ground black pepper

1 Whiz together the peas, goats cheese, mint leaves, garlic, lemon zest and extra virgin olive oil in a food processor until you have a relatively smooth consistency. Add lemon juice and salt and pepper to taste.

2 Spoon into a serving bowl and add a sprinkling of extra mint leaves and / or lemon juice to serve.

A few arugula leaves and some slices of fresh focaccia or ciabatta bread are perfect with this delicious appetizer, whether you serve it warm or cold. For best results, make sure your tomatoes are really ripe and juicy.

Mozzarella-and-Prosciutto-Baked Tomatoes

MAKES 4 adult portions
PREPARATION TIME 15 minutes
COOKING TIME 20 minutes

12 juicy, ripe tomatoes (roughly the size
   of golf balls)
4 ounces buffalo mozzarella, cut into
   12 pieces
2 oregano sprigs
4 slices prosciutto, each torn into
   3 pieces
about 2 tablespoons extra virgin olive oil
sea salt and freshly ground black pepper

TO SERVE
arugula leaves
fresh Italian bread
extra virgin olive oil
balsamic vinegar

1 Heat the oven to 350°F and line a baking sheet with parchment paper or aluminum foil.

2 Cut a cross on the top of each tomato, cutting halfway down, then put them on the prepared baking sheet. Squeeze each tomato very lightly to open it up slightly, then season with salt and pepper. Gently press a piece of mozzarella into each tomato, followed by a couple oregano leaves and a piece of prosciutto. Don't worry if it doesn't all fit in properly at this point, because once the tomatoes are in the oven, the cheese will melt and the ham will fall into place. (If you are serving the tomatoes warm, they can be prepared up to this stage a couple of hours before going into the oven.)

3 Drizzle the extra virgin olive oil over, then bake the tomatoes 15 to 20 minutes until the cheese melts and the prosciutto is starting to color.

4 Serve on individual plates or on a serving platter to share, with peppery arugula leaves and fresh Italian bread and extra virgin olive oil and balsamic vinegar for dipping.

This is such an easy appetizer to prepare and the results are really impressive. Smoked mackerel has a delicious, rich flavor and a texture that is perfectly complemented by the sweet-and-sour beet relish. If you have beets left over from making this relish, try the Beet and Sour Cream Dip on page 171.

Smoked Mackerel and Horseradish Pâté with Beet Relish

MAKES 4 adult portions
PREPARATION TIME 20 minutes

FOR THE SMOKED MACKEREL AND HORSERADISH PÂTÉ
9 ounces skinless smoked mackerel fillets
5 tablespoons sour cream
⅔ cup cream cheese
1 tablespoon hot horseradish sauce
2 teaspoons lemon juice
sea salt and freshly ground black pepper
toast, crispbread or bruschetta, to serve

FOR THE BEET RELISH
1 cup finely diced cooked beet
2 tablespoons bottled caramelized onions
a splash balsamic vinegar
1 tablespoon finely chopped flat-leaf parsley or thyme leaves

1 Flake the mackerel into a food processor, removing any bones you come across. Add the sour cream, cream cheese, horseradish, lemon juice and plenty black pepper. Blend the pâté until smooth. Spoon into four individual dishes, cover with plastic wrap and put in the refrigerator.

2 To make the relish, mix all the ingredients together in a nonmetallic bowl and season with a little salt and pepper. (Both the pâté and the relish can be prepared a day in advance and kept cold in the refrigerator.)

3 Serve the pâté with the relish and toast.

This light and flavorsome soup really has the wow factor—but the wonderful reality is that it's amazingly easy to make. If you want a change from shrimp, try using sliced chicken or tofu instead.

Hot-and-Sour Soup with Shrimp

MAKES 4 adult portions
PREPARATION TIME 10 minutes
COOKING TIME 8 minutes

7 ounces shelled jumbo shrimp
½ teaspoon sea salt
1½ teaspoons sugar
3½ ounces vermicelli rice noodles
4⅓ cups vegetable stock
2 lemongrass stalks
2 tablespoons Thai fish sauce
¼ teaspoon chili paste
1½ cups thinly sliced shiitake
   mushrooms
1 cup halved baby plum tomatoes
4 scallions, thinly sliced
juice of 1½ limes
3 fresh or dried kaffir lime leaves, torn
   into pieces
a few cilantro leaves, for sprinkling

1 Put the shrimp in a small nonmetallic bowl and stir in the salt and ½ teaspoon of the sugar. This will really bring out their flavor. Break the noodles into about 2-inch-long pieces and soak them in hot water a couple minutes to soften. (You can get all the ingredients ready and prepare the recipe to this point, then put everything in the refrigerator so you only have the the last-minute cooking just before serving.)

2 Meanwhile, heat the stock in a wok or large saucepan over medium heat. Bash the ends of the lemongrass to help release their delicious flavor, then add to the pan with the fish sauce, chili paste and remaining sugar. Bring to a boil, then reduce the heat to low and leave to simmer 5 minutes.

3 Drain the noodles and add them to the wok with the shrimp, shiitake mushrooms, tomatoes, scallions, lime juice and kaffir lime leaves. Simmer about 5 minutes until the shrimp turn pink. Have a taste. If the soup can do with being slightly more spicy, add a little more chili paste; if it's a little too hot, add extra sugar and a squeeze of lime.

4 Serve sprinkled with a few cilantro leaves.

As always with chilies, taste and adjust the spiciness to suit what you like best. This is a great way to use up bread that's not super-fresh, or you can make the dish look much more sophisticated by using a fancy, artisan bread. The addition of sumac gives a distinctive tang, but use a squeeze of lemon if you don't have any.

Crab and Chili Toasts

MAKES 4 adult portions
PREPARATION TIME 15 minutes
COOKING TIME 5 minutes

7 ounces fresh white crabmeat
finely grated zest of 1 lemon
1 teaspoon sumac or crushed fennel seeds or a squeeze of lemon juice
2 tablespoons chopped flat-leaf parsley leaves
2 tablespoons extra virgin olive oil, plus extra for drizzling
½ to 1 red chili, seeded and finely chopped
4 to 8 slices ciabatta or sourdough bread (depending on the size)
sea salt and freshly ground black pepper
watercress or arugula leaves, to serve

1 Put the white crabmeat in a nonmetallic bowl and break up any chunks with your fingers or a fork. Add the lemon zest, sumac, parsley and extra virgin olive oil and season lightly with salt and pepper. (The crab mixture can be made several hours before you need it, covered and kept cold in the refrigerator.)

2 Heat the broiler to high. Drizzle the bread with extra virgin olive oil, then lightly toast it under the broiler. If they are particularly large slices of bread, cut them in half. Spoon the crab mixture onto the toasts and serve with a little watercress or arugula.

Leftovers for lemon-spiced vegetables
sautéed potatoes with sumac and thyme
An open jar of sumac can be used in a variety of ways, but one that creates a real wow factor is to fry **slices of leftover boiled potatoes** in a combination of **olive oil** and **butter** until they are becoming golden and crisp. Add a good sprinkling of **sumac** and some **thyme leaves**. Continue to fry a few minutes longer before seasoning with **sea salt** and **freshly ground black pepper**. Serve with **fish**, **chicken** or simply topped with **a fried egg**.

Serve this delicious dish hot or chilled, depending on the weather. It's also always a great favorite with the kids—they love the sweet flavor from the peas and the creamy texture—so it is worth making more than you need and freezing the extra for a later date.

Pea and Watercress Soup with Tomato and Mint Salsa

MAKES 4 adult portions
PREPARATION TIME 15 minutes
COOKING TIME 10 minutes

FOR THE PEA AND WATERCRESS SOUP
2 tablespoons olive oil
1 leek, sliced
3½ cups chicken or vegetable stock
4 cups frozen peas
3½ ounces watercress
7 tablespoons cream cheese
sea salt and freshly ground black pepper

FOR THE TOMATO AND MINT SALSA
4 ripe tomatoes, seeded and diced
4 scallions, chopped
1 handful mint leaves, chopped
1 tablespoon extra virgin olive oil
a small squeeze lemon juice

1 Heat the oil in a saucepan over low heat, add the leek and fry about 5 minutes until it is soft but not colored. Add the stock and bring to a boil, then add the peas and watercress. Return to a boil and boil 3 minutes, or until the peas are tender. Stir in the cream cheese and season with salt and pepper.

2 Blitz the soup in a food processor or blender, or by using a hand blender, until it is smooth. Check for seasoning and add extra, if needed. (Prepare the soup up to a day in advance up to this stage, cool and keep chilled until you are ready to finish and serve.)

3 To make the salsa, mix together all the salsa ingredients and season with salt and pepper.

4 Serve the soup hot or chilled, with the tomato salsa spooned over each bowl.

This is a fantastic combination of flavors that make a light and stylish appetizer. If you have room to grow a few herbs in the garden, that's great, because you'll always have fresh supplies to hand. If not, keep a few growing in pots on the windowsill if you can.

Roasted Mushroom Brioches with Goat Cheese

MAKES 4 adult portions
PREPARATION TIME 15 minutes
COOKING TIME 20 minutes

5 tablespoons butter, at room temperature
2 tablespoons chopped oregano leaves or 1 tablespoon chopped thyme leaves, plus extra leaves for sprinkling
2 plump garlic cloves, crushed
finely grated zest of ½ lemon
1 brioche loaf (about 7 ounces)
4 large, flat white or cremini mushrooms (about 5 inches in diameter)
5 ounces mild soft goat cheese
extra virgin olive oil, for drizzling
sea salt and freshly ground black pepper

1 Heat the oven to 400°F and line a baking sheet with parchment paper.

2 Mix together the butter, oregano, garlic, lemon zest, salt and pepper.

3 Cut 4 slices of brioche, each about 1¼ inches thick. Spread half the herb butter onto one side of each piece of brioche. Top each one with a mushroom, stem-side up, then spread the remaining butter over the mushrooms. (The mushroom brioches can be prepared to this stage several hours before they are needed. Cover with plastic wrap and keep in a cool place.)

4 Put the mushroom brioche on the prepared baking sheet and roast 15 to 20 minutes until the mushrooms are tender and the brioches are golden brown.

5 Top each mushroom with a spoonful of goat cheese, drizzle with extra virgin olive oil and add a twist of black pepper, then sprinkle with oregano or thyme leaves and serve.

Leftovers for breakfast
hot jam brioche sandwich
For a comforting breakfast treat, sandwich a **couple of slices of brioche** together with **1 tablespoon jam** or **marmalade**. Beat **1 egg** with **2 teaspoons sugar** (plain, vanilla or cinnamon) and soak the brioche in the egg until all the egg is absorbed. Fry in **melted butter** 1 to 2 minutes on each side until golden. Sprinkle with **sugar** and enjoy.

Halloumi cheese, originally from Cyprus, is a firm cheese with a strong, salty flavor that is more than a match for the spices in this recipe—in fact, you can say it's a match made in heaven!

Spicy Halloumi with Tomato and Cilantro Salad

MAKES 4 adult portions
PREPARATION TIME 15 minutes, plus
  2 hours marinating
COOKING TIME 8 minutes

FOR THE SPICY HALLOUMI
13 ounces halloumi cheese, cut into
  ½-inch slices
2 tablespoons olive oil
2 teaspoons garam masala
½ teaspoon chili powder
a squeeze lemon juice

FOR THE TOMATO AND CILANTRO SALAD
2 cups halved cherry tomatoes
½ red onion, thinly sliced
2 tablespoons extra virgin olive oil
1 tablespoon lemon juice
1 handful cilantro leaves, chopped
sea salt and freshly ground black pepper

TO SERVE
4 tablespoons plain yogurt or Cucumber
  Raita (see page 25; optional)
warmed mini naan bread (optional)

1 Put the halloumi cheese in a nonmetallic bowl or sandwich bag. Mix together the olive oil, garam masala, chili powder and lemon juice. Pour over the halloumi and gently turn the cheese so it is coated in the spiced oil. Cover and leave the cheese to marinate in the refrigerator 2 hours so it absorbs the flavors. (Ideally, the halloumi needs a couple of hours in the spiced oil; you can leave it in the refrigerator all day if that's more convenient.)

2 Meanwhile, to make the salad, toss together the tomatoes, onion, extra virgin olive oil, lemon juice and cilantro in a nonmetallic bowl. Season lightly with salt and pepper.

3 To cook the halloumi, heat a large ridged griddle or skillet over medium-high heat, add the halloumi and fry a couple of minutes on each side until golden brown. You might need to do this in batches; if so, put the hot halloumi on a plate and keep warm by covering loosely with foil while you cook the remainder.

4 Serve the halloumi alongside the salad with the yogurt or raita and naan bread, if you like.

Leftovers for an Indian-style lunch
mini naan "pizzas"
If you plan to serve mini naan bread with this appetizer, grab an extra package and make quick Indian-inspired pizzas for the kids. Mix **1 tablespoon mild curry paste** and **1 tablespoon mango chutney** into ½ **can (15-oz.) crushed tomatoes**. Spread this mixture over the top of **2 or 4 naan bread** (depending on their size). Top with **crumbled feta cheese**, and a sprinkling each of **thawed peas** and **chopped scallions**. Drizzle with **a little olive oil**, then bake in an oven heated to 425°F about 10 minutes.

A special thanks goes to my friend Mai-yee for this recipe, the perfect appetizer for any oriental meal. The ingredients are readily available in supermarkets or oriental food stores. You will need white miso paste, because there's no substitute, but you can use dry sherry for sake, very sweet sherry or 1 tablespoon rice wine with 1 teaspoon dissolved sugar for mirin, and vegetable or chicken stock for dashi, if necessary.

Baked Miso Eggplant

MAKES 4 adult portions
PREPARATION TIME 5 minutes
COOKING TIME 35 minutes

1 tablespoon sake
1 tablespoon mirin
5 tablespoons white miso paste
1 egg yolk
1 tablespoon sugar
4 tablespoons dashi stock
2 eggplants
sunflower oil, for brushing
sesame oil, for drizzling

TO SERVE
2 teaspoons toasted sesame seeds
4 scallions, thinly sliced
½ red chili, seeded and thinly sliced

1 Heat the oven to 400°F and line a baking sheet with parchment paper.

2 Put the sake and mirin in a small saucepan over medium heat and bring just to a boil. Boil about 30 seconds for the alcohol to burn off. Reduce the heat to low and, using a small whisk, mix in the miso, egg yolk and sugar. Add the stock and simmer gently about 5 minutes, stirring frequently, until you have the consistency of custard sauce. Remove the pan from the heat. (This thick miso sauce can be made a day ahead, left to cool and kept covered in the refrigerator.)

3 Cut the eggplants in half lengthwise and, using a small, sharp knife, diagonally score lines into the flesh, about ½ inch apart, to form a lattice pattern, taking care not to cut all the way through. Brush both sides of the eggplant with the sunflower oil and put, cut-side down, on the prepared baking sheet. Bake the eggplants 15 minutes, then turn them over, return the baking sheet to the oven and bake the eggplants 10 minutes longer, or until they are soft and lightly colored.

4 Heat the broiler to high. Remove the eggplants from the oven and drizzle with sesame oil. Spread the miso sauce over the top, then broil just a couple of minutes until the sauce bubbles.

5 Serve hot, scattered with the sesame seeds, scallions and red chili, and enjoy straightaway.

Lifesavers for oriental recipes
sake, mirin and miso marinade
Once you buy these ingredients you'll find many uses for them in stir-fries and marinades for a variety of oriental recipes. A flavorsome marinade I like to make is to mix together **4 tablespoons sake**, **4 tablespoons mirin**, **½ cup white miso paste** and **¼ cup plus 1 tablespoon sugar**. This can be used to marinate chicken or fish (at least 24 hours) before broiling or roasting. Both kids and adults will love the sweet flavor it creates.

Packed with plenty of flavors, this deliciously simple dish includes coconut milk for a rich finish. You can make the whole recipe a day or two in advance, or split up the stages, marinating the chicken and making the tomato sauce a day before you need the dish and then finishing the cooking the next day.

South Indian Chicken Curry

MAKES 4 adult portions
PREPARATION TIME 15 minutes, plus at least 10 minutes marinating
COOKING TIME 1 hour

8 to12 boneless, skinless chicken thighs (depending on size)
1 teaspoon turmeric
1 teaspoon ground coriander
1 teaspoon cayenne pepper
½ teaspoon coarsely and freshly ground black pepper
juice of 1 lemon
4 tablespoons sunflower oil
1 teaspoon black mustard seeds
2 large pinches dried curry leaves
1 large onion, sliced
¾-inch piece gingerroot, peeled and grated
3 garlic cloves, crushed
1 can (15-oz.) crushed tomatoes
1¾ cups canned coconut milk
1½ tablespoons tamarind paste
1 handful cilantro leaves, roughly chopped
sea salt

TO SERVE
Perfect Basmati Rice (see page 14)
naan bread (optional)

1 Put the chicken in a large freezer bag. Mix together the turmeric, ground coriander, chili powder, black pepper and lemon juice, then pour over the chicken. Seal the bag and mix everything together. Leave to marinate in the refrigerator at least 10 minutes, but, for the best flavor, an hour or longer is preferable.

2 Heat 2 tablespoons of the oil in a saucepan over medium heat and add the mustard seeds and curry leaves. When the mustard seeds begin to pop, stir in the onion. Cover and cook 10 to 15 minutes, stirring occasionally. Add the gingerroot and garlic and cook a couple minutes longer. Stir in the tomatoes and ¾ cup plus 2 tablespoons water. The best thing to do is half fill the empty tomato can with water and pour straight into the pan. Bring to a boil, then reduce the heat and leave to simmer about 15 minutes.

3 Meanwhile, heat the remaining oil in a large wok with a lid, a saucepan or a Dutch oven over medium heat. When it is almost smoking, add the marinated chicken, with any leftover marinade, and fry about 8 minutes until the chicken is colored all over. Stir in the tomato sauce, coconut milk, tamarind and a good pinch salt. Bring to a boil, then reduce the heat and leave to simmer 25 to 30 minutes until the chicken is tender and cooked through and the sauce is thick. Stir in the cilantro and serve with rice and naan bread, if you like.

This is a simple summery recipe that can easily be transformed into a vegetarian dish by swapping the duck for sliced, pan-fried halloumi cheese. The lentil salad also is delicious the following day, and if you mix it with crumbled feta, it makes a perfect packed lunch or quick, healthy snack.

Honey and Cinnamon Duck with Lentil and Pomegranate Salad

MAKES 4 adult portions
PREPARATION TIME 15 minutes
COOKING TIME 18 minutes

FOR THE HONEY AND CINNAMON DUCK
4 duck breast halves, skin on
2 teaspoons cinnamon
2 tablespoons olive oil
3 tablespoons honey
sea salt and freshly ground black pepper

FOR THE LENTIL AND POMEGRANATE SALAD
2½ cups cooked Puy lentils (see below)
1 red onion, thinly sliced
½ bag (10-oz) baby spinach leaves
1 small bunch mint, roughly chopped
1 pomegranate (or ½ cup prepared seeds)
juice of 1 lemon
3 tablespoons extra virgin olive oil
½ teaspoon ground cumin
½ teaspoon ground coriander
½ cup toasted almonds

FOR THE SPICED YOGURT
1 to 2 teaspoons harissa paste
6 tablespoons Greek yogurt

1 Heat the oven to 375°F.

2 Using a sharp knife, score the duck skin several times, then rub the cinnamon and some salt and pepper into the skin and meat. Heat the oil in an ovenproof skillet over medium heat, add the duck breasts, skin-side down, and fry 10 minutes, or until crisp. Drain off the fat, turn the duck breasts over and drizzle the honey over the skins. Transfer the skillet to the oven and roast the duck breasts 8 minutes, then remove them from the pan and leave to rest in a warm place at least 5 minutes.

3 In a large bowl, mix together the lentils, onion, spinach leaves and mint. Cut the pomegranates in half and, holding each half over the bowl, bash the outer skin with a wooden spoon until all the seeds fall into the bowl. You'll need to bash the skin a few times before the seeds begin to fall out, but they will. Mix the ingredients together.

4 In a separate bowl, mix together the lemon juice, extra virgin olive oil, cumin and coriander and season with salt and pepper. Pour this mixture over the salad and mix well. Sprinkle with the almonds. Mix together the harissa paste and yogurt.

5 Serve the duck breasts whole or sliced, with the lentil salad and spiced yogurt.

How to cook

puy lentils

Cans of ready-to-eat Puy lentils are an ideal time-saver for this recipe, but if you want to cook the lentils from scratch, here's how to do it. To make 2½ cups cooked lentils, rinse **1¼ cups dry Puy lentils** under running water. Put them in a saucepan and cover with 3 times their volume (about **3¾ cups**) **hot vegetable stock**. Bring to a boil, then reduce the heat and leave to simmer 20 to 25 minutes, or perhaps a little longer, until just tender. Drain and serve straightaway or leave them to cool.

Crisp Pork Belly with Warm Bean, Fennel and Apple Salad

MAKES 4 adult portions
PREPARATION TIME 25 minutes,
  plus 30 minutes resting
COOKING TIME 3 hours

FOR THE PORK
3-pound-12-ounce-piece boneless
  pork belly, scored
2 teaspoons flaked sea salt
olive oil, for drizzling
2 teaspoons fennel seeds, crushed
juice of 1 lemon

**FOR THE WARM BEAN, FENNEL AND
  APPLE SALAD**
2 tablespoons olive oil
2 fennel bulbs, thinly sliced
2 cups green beans cut into short pieces
2 red apples, cored and cut into ½-inch
  chunks
a pinch dried chili flakes
2 cans (15-oz.) navy or cannellini beans,
  drained
¾ cup plus 2 tablespoons chicken stock
a squeeze of lemon juice
sea salt and freshly ground black pepper

1 For really crisp crackling, rub the pork skin generously with the salt, put the pork skin-side down on a wire rack in a roasting pan, cover and leave in the refrigerator overnight to draw out the excess moisture.

2 Heat the oven to 475°F. Pat the pork dry with paper towels. Put it back skin-side up in the roasting pan. Drizzle a little olive oil over the skin, then rub in the fennel seeds and sea salt, making sure they go down between the score lines. Put the pork belly in the oven and roast 30 minutes.

3 Pour the lemon juice over the meat. Reduce the oven temperature to 315°F and roast 1½ to 2 hours longer until the meat is meltingly soft and the skin wonderfully crisp. Check twice during the time that the pork fat and juices are not burning on the bottom of the pan. If they are, just add a cup of water. Continue roasting the pork if you want the skin even crispier; it won't do the meat any harm. Transfer the pork to a board, cover loosely with aluminum foil and leave to rest in a warm place up to 30 minutes.

4 When you are almost ready to serve, throw together the warm salad. Heat the oil in a large skillet over medium heat, add the fennel and green beans and fry about 8 minutes until just they are just tender. Add the apples and chili flakes and cook about 2 minutes longer until the apples are just tender. Stir in the navy beans and stock. Bring to a boil, then reduce the heat and leave to simmer 2 minutes, or until the beans are heated through. Season lightly with sea salt, freshly ground pepper and a squeeze of lemon juice.

5 Using a serrated knife, cut the pork into thick slices, then serve with the warm bean salad.

Leftovers for tortillas
pork and hoisin wrap
Use two forks to shred any **leftover pork**. Spread **a wheat tortilla** with **1 tablespoon hoisin sauce**, then top with the pork, **shredded crisp lettuce**, **chopped scallions** and **matchsticks of cucumber**. Roll up and enjoy straightaway, or, if you're making it for a packed lunch, wrap in wax paper with the ends twisted to seal together.

This is a delicious North African dish that is ideally suited to serving with couscous or flatbread. You need two really juicy lemons—buy the unwaxed ones if you can. This is also a great dish to choose for a dinner party because you can make it a day ahead.

Moroccan Lamb Meatballs with Olives and Lemon

MAKES 4 adult portions
PREPARATION TIME 20 minutes
COOKING TIME 40 minutes

3 onions, quartered
1 pound 2 ounces ground lamb
1 teaspoon ground cinnamon
1 teaspoon ground cumin
½ teaspoon cayenne pepper
finely grated zest and juice of 1 lemon, plus 1 lemon, cut into wedges
1 handful flat-leaf parsley leaves, chopped
2 tablespoons olive oil
1 red chilli, seeded and finely chopped
2 tablespoons peeled and grated or finely chopped gingerroot
a large pinch saffron strands
1 cup plus 2 tablespooons lamb stock
2 tablespoons tomato paste
¾ cup ripe or green kalamata olives, pitted
1 small handful cilantro leaves, chopped
sea salt and freshly ground black pepper
couscous or flatbread, to serve

1 Put the onions in a food processor and whiz until finely chopped. Remove half and set aside. Add the lamb, spices, lemon zest, parsley and salt and pepper to the food processor and whiz to combine. Tip out the mixture and, using wet hands to stop the mixture sticking to you, shape it into walnut-size balls. (The meatballs can be made a day before cooking and kept in the refrigerator. Or, to be really prepared, they can be frozen up to 3 months.)

2 Heat the oil in a large Dutch oven over medium heat, add the reserved onion, the chili, ginger and saffron and cook about 5 minutes until the onion is soft and starting to color. Add the lemon juice, stock, tomato paste and olives and bring to a boil. Add the meatballs, reduce the heat and cover with a lid. Simmer the meatballs 20 minutes. (You can make the recipe to this point the day before, then finish it from here when you like.)

3 Remove the lid and add the coriander and lemon wedges, tucking them into the dish. Cook, uncovered, 10 minutes longer until the liquid reduces and thickens slightly.

4 Serve hot with couscous or flatbread.

Bulgur wheat or brown rice go really well with this delicious dish of meltingly tender lamb with that wonderful sweet-spicy combination characteristic of Middle Eastern cuisine. But the best thing about this recipe is you can cook it a day ahead, making it the ideal dinner party dish when you know you'll have very little time to cook on the actual day.

Persian Lamb Stew

MAKES 4 adult portions
PREPARATION TIME 15 minutes
COOKING TIME 2¼ hours

⅔ cup walnut halves or pieces
2 tablespoons olive oil
2 onions, sliced
2 garlic cloves, crushed
2 pounds boneless lamb shoulder, diced
½ teaspoon turmeric
½ teaspoon ground cinnamon
1 cup dried cranberries
2 cups plus 3 tablespoons lamb stock
4 tablespoons pomegranate molasses
1 small bunch flat-leaf parsley, chopped
sea salt and freshly ground black pepper

1 Heat the oven to 300°F.

2 Put the walnuts on a baking sheet and place in the oven 10 minutes, or until toasted. Leave to cool slightly, then tip into a sandwich bag and bash with a rolling pin to crush finely, or chop them on a cutting board.

3 Heat the oil in a large Dutch oven over medium heat, add the onions and fry 10 minutes, or until soft and golden. Increase the heat to high, add the garlic and lamb and cook until brown all over. Stir in the spices and cook about 1 minute. Mix in the cranberries, stock, pomegranate molasses and walnuts. Cover with a lid and place in the oven 1½ hours.

4 Remove the lid and cook 15 to 30 minutes longer until the sauce thickens slightly. (The stew can be cooked to this point at least a day beforehand and gently reheated when needed.)

5 Season to taste with salt and pepper, stir in the parsley and serve.

Leftovers for dessert
pomegranate and yogurt puddings
This is a refreshing dessert to serve after the Persian Lamb Stew. To serve 4, layer the **segments of 3 oranges**, **2 tablespoons roughly chopped pistachios**, **1 cup plus 2 tablespoons Greek yogurt** and **drizzles of pomegranate molasses** (roughly **1 tablespoon** per serving) in glasses or small dishes. Finish with **a scattering of pistachios** and **mint sprigs** to decorate.

This delicious Indonesian coconut and beef curry needs to simmer about three hours, which gives you plenty of time to get on with doing the one hundred things you have to do before people start arriving.

Beef Rendang

MAKES 4 adult portions
PREPARATION TIME 20 minutes
COOKING TIME 3½ hours

4 shallots, roughly chopped
3 garlic cloves
1¼-inch piece gingerroot, peeled and
   roughly chopped
3 red chilies, 2 seeded and all 3 roughly
   chopped
¾-inch piece galangal (if available,
   if not, add a little more gingerroot)
1 lemongrass stalk, outer layer removed
   and the rest roughly chopped
1 teaspoon ground turmeric
1½ teaspoon sea salt
2¼ pounds stewing or casserole beef
3½ cups canned coconut milk
3 kaffir lime leaves (fresh or dried),
   chopped or crushed

FOR THE TOMATO AND CILANTRO SALSA
3 ripe tomatoes, quartered, seeded and
   finely diced
¼ cucumber, finely diced
1 small red onion, finely chopped
1 handful cilantro leaves, chopped
juice of ½ lime
1½ tablespoons olive oil
sea salt and freshly ground black pepper

TO SERVE
lime wedges
boiled or steamed Thai Jasmine rice

1 Put the shallots, garlic, ginger, chilies, galangal, if using, lemongrass, turmeric and salt in a blender or food processor and add ⅔ cup water. Blitz to a smooth paste.

2 Put the spice paste in a large wok or saucepan, add the beef, coconut milk and lime leaves. Top up with water if the meat is not quite covered. Stir well and bring to a boil, then reduce the heat to very low and leave to gently bubble away, uncovered, 3 to 3½ hours, stirring occasionally.

3 Make the salsa by mixing together the tomatoes, cucumber, onion and cilantro. Keep in the refrigerator until you are ready to serve. (You can make this a several hours ahead, if you like.)

4 When the dish is ready, the coconut milk will have reduced, with the oil starting to appear on the surface, and the curry will be fairly thick. (This dish can be cooked the day before you plan to serve it, then gently reheated when needed.)

5 Drizzle the lime juice and olive oil over the salsa, season with salt and pepper and toss together.

6 Serve the beef hot with lime wedges, Thai rice and the tomato salsa.

All my friends and family love a fish pie so I make extra for the kids whenever I make this. For variety from a more-traditional potato-topping, however, I make this with a crunchy, cheesy topping, and it is always popular. As an added bonus, the crumb topping is quicker and easier to make than boiling and mashing potaoes. I like to serve this with a simple green salad.

Salmon and Shrimp Crumble

MAKES 4 adult and 2 child portions
PREPARATION TIME 20 minutes
COOKING TIME 55 minutes

FOR THE FILLING
5 tablespoons butter
1 onion, chopped
1 bay leaf
½ cup all-purpose flour
⅔ cup white wine
¾ cup plus 2 tablespoons milk
1 pound 10 ounces salmon fillet, skinned and cut into 1¼-inch cubes
10 ounces shelled jumbo shrimp
3 eggs, hard-boiled, shelled and chopped
2 tablespoons chopped dill
2 tablespoons capers, rinsed
sea salt and freshly ground black pepper

FOR THE CRUMBLE TOPPING
1 ciabatta loaf, about 7 ounces
¼ cup finely grated fresh Parmesan cheese
3 tablespoons olive oil
2 tablespoons chopped parsley leaves

1 Heat the oven to 400°F.

2 Melt the butter in a large saucepan over medium heat, add the onion and the bay leaf and fry until the onion is soft but not colored. Stir in the flour and continue stirring about 30 seconds, then gradually add the wine, stirring to prevent any floury lumps, then finally stir in the milk. Bring to a boil, then reduce the heat and simmer a few minutes, still stirring, until you have a thick sauce. Stir in the salmon and shrimp and cook a few minutes until the shrimp turn pink. Add the eggs and dill, and season with salt and pepper.

3 Spoon most of the mixture into a large baking dish suitable to serve from and scatter the capers over. Divide the remaining filling between two small baking dish for the kids. You can add extra capers to theirs, too, if you think they will like them.

4 To make the topping, tear the ciabatta bread into pieces, put in a food processor and blitz to form rough crumbs. Add the Parmesan, oil and parsley, then briefly blitz again to combine. (The filling and crumbs can be made a day in advance and kept in the refrigerator.)

5 When you are ready to cook the fish pie, scatter the topping over the filling, put the dish on a cookie sheet and bake 30 to 40 minutes (or slightly longer if you are cooking the filling from chilled) until the topping is golden and the filling is bubbling at the edges. Serve the crumble piping hot.

Thai Tuna Fish Cakes with Sweet-and-Sour Dipping Sauce and Rice Salad

MAKES 4 adult portions
PREPARATION TIME 30 minutes
COOKING TIME 6 minutes

FOR THE RICE SALAD
1½ cups Thai Jasmine rice or basmati
    rice
4 tablespoons rice vinegar
2 tablespoons sugar
1 bunch scallions, thinly sliced
1 red bell pepper, seeded and thinly
    sliced
½ cucumber, halved lengthwise, seeded
    and thinly sliced
1 large handful each basil, mint and
    cilantro leaves
sea salt

FOR THE THAI TUNA FISH CAKES
1 pound 5 ounces fresh tuna
1½ tablespoons Thai red curry paste
1½ tablespoons Thai fish sauce
1 handful cilantro leaves
4 scallions, roughly chopped
1 egg, lightly beaten
sunflower oil, for frying

**FOR THE SWEET-AND-SOUR DIPPING
    SAUCE**
1 red chili, seeded and finely chopped
4 tablespoons rice vinegar
4 teaspoons ugar
½-inch piece gingerroot, peeled and
    grated
2 tablespoons finely chopped cilantro
    leaves

1 To make the salad, put the rice in a saucepan with a pinch salt and 1¾ cups water. Bring to a boil, then cover with a tight-fitting lid, reduce the heat to low and leave the rice to simmer 10 minutes. Remove the pan from the heat but don't lift the lid. Leave the rice to stand 5 to 10 minutes.

2 Fluff up the rice with a fork, tip it out onto a baking sheet, loosely spreading it out so it cools, then set aside 5 minutes, or until it reaches room temperature. Put in the refrigerator to chill.

3 Once the rice is cold, transfer it to a large bowl. Gently heat the rice vinegar, sugar and a pinch salt in a small pan, stirring until the sugar dissolves. Stir into the rice with the scallions, red pepper, cucumber and herbs. The salad is ready.

4 Put all the fish cake ingredients in a food processor and blitz briefly to make a smooth paste. Using wet hands to stop the mixture sticking to you, divide into about 12 equal balls and flatten each one lightly to form a patty.

5 Mix together all the ingredients for the dipping sauce. (You can prepare everything to this point several hours in advance and keep the refrigerator.)

6 Heat about ½ inch oil in a skillet over medium heat, add the fish cakes and fry, in batches, about 3 minutes on each side until golden brown. Drain on paper towels and keep warm, if necessary, until you finish frying all the fish cakes, then serve them with the rice salad and a bowl of dipping sauce.

Leftovers transformed
simple sushi
Making sushi is much simpler than you might think. Chill any leftover **rice salad** well. With wet hands, gently shape a ball of rice the size of a small egg into an oblong. Snip large pieces of **red bell pepper** or **cucumber** with scissors. Dot a little **wasabi paste** (or mayonnaise) on the surface and finish by topping with a **cooked shrimp**, **smoked salmon**, a **crab stick**, **canned tuna** mashed with **mayonnaise**, **sliced avocado**, a **cooked asparagus tip** or, if you just happen to have any, **slices of fresh salmon** or **tuna**. Serve with **soy sauce**, **wasabi** and **pickled ginger** for a proper sushi experience.

To save a huge amount of time and effort, this recipe has a secret short cut: it uses a can of seafood soup as the base. But if you don't tell anyone, they will never know.

Effortless Bouillabaisse

MAKES 4 adult portions
PREPARATION TIME 20 minutes
COOKING TIME 20 minutes

FOR THE BOUILLABAISSE
2 tablespoons olive oil
2 leeks, thinly sliced
1 can (14-oz.) cherry tomatoes
1¾ cups canned lobster or seafood
  bisque
2 strips orange zest
a large pinch dried chili flakes
a small splash brandy
2 pounds 4 ounces white fish, such
  as monkfish, cod, pollack, haddock
  or sea bass, cut into bite-size pieces
8 to 12 whole large shrimp
1 tablespoon chopped flat-leaf parsley
  leaves
1 tablespoon snipped chives
sea salt and freshly ground black pepper

FOR THE TOAST
8 slices French bread, for toasting
extra virgin olive oil, for drizzling
6 tablespoons garlic mayonnaise
1 teaspoon harissa paste

1 Heat the olive oil in a large saucepan over medium heat, add the leeks and fry a few minutes until they are soft but not colored. Add the tomatoes, bisque, orange zest, chili flakes, brandy and ⅔ cup water. Bring to a boil, then reduce the heat and leave to simmer 5 minutes. Stir the fish into the pan, and simmer 8 minutes longer. Add the shrimp, stirring in gently. Return the liquid to a simmer and simmer about 3 minutes until the shrimp turn pink.

2 Meanwhile, heat the broiler to high. To make the toast, drizzle the bread with a little extra virgin olive oil, then lightly toast on both sides. Mix together the garlic mayonnaise and harissa paste. Either spread the spiced mayonnaise on the toast or spoon it into a bowl.

3 Once all the fish is cooked, season lightly with salt and pepper and remove the orange zest strips if you can find them. Scatter with the parsley and chives.

4 Spoon the bouillabaisse into bowls and serve with the toast and garlic mayonnaise.

Leftovers for a marinade
harissa and yogurt marinade
If you are stuck for a quick-and-simple way to liven up chicken breasts or fish fillets during the week, grab your open jar of harissa and try this. Mix together **2 teaspoons harissa, 2 tablespoons Greek** or **plain yogurt,** the **grated zest and juice of ½ lemon**, **½ teaspoon ground cumin** and **a pinch salt**. Spread or rub all over **2 scored chicken breast halves** or **2 fish fillets** or **2 steaks**, cover and leave to marinate in the refrigerator for anything between 10 minutes and 24 hours.

This is my idea of a real-life recipe: a paella dish that doesn't require you to invest in a vast skillet, or expect you to be fiddling about in the kitchen while your guests catch up on the must-hear gossip.

Baked Seafood Paella

MAKES 4 adult portions
PREPARATION TIME 20 minutes
COOKING TIME 30 minutes

3 tablespoons olive oil
1 onion, chopped
2 garlic cloves, crushed
1 red bell pepper, seeded and sliced
1½ cups paella rice
1 cup plus 2 tablespoons dry white wine
a large pinch saffron strands
1 teaspoon smoked Spanish paprika
   or standard sweet paprika
3¼ cups hot fish or chicken stock
1 pounds 2 ounces live shellfish, such
   as mussels and / or clams
2 squid tubes, cut into rings
1 cup frozen peas, thawed, or chopped
   fresh green beans
8 to 12 raw whole, large shrimp
½ small bunch flat-leaf parsley, chopped
1 lemon, cut into wedges
sea salt and freshly ground black pepper

1 Scrub the mussels thoroughly with a stiff brush under cold running water to remove all traces of grit, then remove any barnacles or other debris attached to the shells and pull off and discard any beards. Rinse again and discard any mussels that stay open.

2 Heat the oven to 425°F.

3 Heat the oil in a large Dutch oven over medium heat, add the onion, garlic and red pepper and fry about 5 minutes until the onion is soft. Add the rice and stir a minute or so until it is coated in the oil, then add the wine, saffron, paprika and stock. Stir well and bring to a boil, then place the Dutch oven in the oven and bake the paella, uncovered, 15 minutes.

4 Stir in the mussels and / or clams, squid and peas and season lightly with salt and pepper. Nestle the shrimp into the surface. Return the Dutch oven to the oven and cook 10 minutes longer, or until the rice is tender and the seafood is cooked through. Make sure all the shrimp are pink and discard any closed mussel or clam shells.

5 Sprinkle the parsley over and serve with lemon wedges. Provide empty bowls for the shells, and a few finger bowls of warm water and plenty of napkins for messy fingers.

How to make
paella mixta

If your friends aren't hugely into seafood, then make your paella with chicken and chorizo. Add **15 ounces thickly sliced or chopped chorizo** and **4 roughly chopped boneless chicken thighs** to the **fried onion** and cook until the chicken is golden brown. Add the **rice** and follow the recipe as above, but just using **shrimp** and not the mussels or squid.

A bowl of fluffy basmati rice and Cucumber Raita (see page 25) make the perfect dishes to serve with this medium-hot curry. For a milder flavor, remove the chili seeds before chopping.

Healthy Vegetable Dhansak

MAKES 4 adult portions
PREPARATION TIME 25 minutes
COOKING TIME 45 minutes

1 cup red lentils
1 large onion
4 garlic cloves
3 green chilies, stems removed
1-inch piece gingerroot, peeled
3 tablespoons sunflower oil
2 sweet potatoes, peeled and cut into bite-size cubes
2 large carrots, peeled and diced
2 red bell peppers, seeded and finely chopped
1¼ cups golden raisins
½ teaspoon turmeric
1 teaspoon ground cumin
1 teaspoon ground coriander
4⅓ cups hot vegetable stock
2 tablespoons tomato paste
4 large ripe tomatoes, each cut into 8 wedges
1½ cups halved green beans
2 teaspoons garam masala
1 small bunch cilantro, chopped
sea salt
pickles or condiments of your choice, to serve

1 Put the lentils in a bowl of cold water and leave to soak about 3 minutes. Drain and leave to one side.

2 Put the onion, garlic, chilies and ginger in a food processor and pulse until finely chopped.

3 Heat the oil in a large saucepan over medium heat, add the onion mixture and fry about 5 minutes until it is starting to become soft and golden. Add the sweet potatoes, carrots and red peppers and fry about 5 minutes. Stir in the golden raisins, turmeric, cumin and coriander and continue frying about 1 minute. Add the drained lentils, hot stock, tomato paste and tomatoes. Stir well and cover with a lid. Simmer 20 minutes, stirring a couple of times. (The dhansak can be cooked up to this stage and removed from the heat at least 2 hours before needed. Simply return to the simmer and continue cooking for the final 10 to 15 minutes in the next step before serving.)

4 Add the green beans and garam masala, then simmer with the lid off 10 to 15 minutes longer until all the vegetables are tender. Sprinkle with the cilantro.

5 Season with a pinch salt and serve as it is or with pickles or condiments of your choice.

Leftovers for a liquid lunch
dhansak soup

Any leftover dhansak is great made into a soup. All you need to do is blend or puree the leftover lentils and vegetables with enough **vegetable stock** to loosen to a soup consistency, then heat gently until simmering. Adjust the seasoning with **salt**, if needed, and serve. I like to fry **sliced onions** and a **few black mustard seeds** in **sunflower oil** until the onions are soft, golden and sweet to spoon on top of the soup.

Quinoa, Beet, Squash and Feta Salad

MAKES 4 adult portions
PREPARATION TIME 25 minutes, plus cooling
COOKING TIME 50 minutes

FOR THE QUINOA, BEET, SQUASH AND FETA SALAD
1 butternut squash, peeled, seeded and cut into bite-size pieces
4 raw beets, cut into bite-size pieces
2 tablespoons olive oil
½ cup less 1 tablespoon hazelnuts
½ cup quinoa
½ bag (10-oz.) baby spinach leaves
1 small bunch mint leaves, roughly chopped
1 bunch scallions, thinly sliced
1 red chili, seeded and thinly sliced
1⅔ cups crumbled feta cheese
sea salt and freshly ground black pepper

FOR THE HONEY AND MUSTARD DRESSING
4 tablespoons canola oil
2 tablespoons honey
2 tablespoons white wine vinegar
1 tablespoon Dijon mustard
finely grated zest of 1 orange

1 Heat the oven to 400°F.

2 Put the butternut squash and beets in a roasting pan, toss with the oil and season lightly with salt and pepper. Roast the beets 40 to 50 minutes until they are soft and beginning to color. Remove them from the oven and leave to cool to room temperature.

3 While you are roasting the vegetables, put the hazelnuts in a small baking sheet and roast 8 minutes, or until golden brown. Leave to cool slightly, then roughly chop and set aside.

4 Rinse the quinoa in cold water, then put in a saucepan with 1¼ cups cold water and a pinch salt. Bring to a boil, then reduce the heat and leave to simmer 20 minutes, or until all the water is absorbed and the quinoa is light and fluffy. Leave to cool.

5 Put the dressing ingredients in a screw-top jar, cover and shake well, then set aside. (You can roast the vegetables and nuts, make the dressing and cook the quinoa several hours in advance. Cover and keep in the refrigerator until you are ready to finish.)

6 To finish, put all the ingredients, except the hazelnuts and feta, in a bowl, then pour the dressing over and toss together. Serve sprinkled with the feta and hazelnuts.

Leftovers for a vegetarian lunch
quinoa with ratatouille
It is a good idea to cook extra quinoa to serve with ratatouille or roasted vegetables. If the kids like couscous, they should enjoy it; it has a slightly nuttier flavor, and is really good for you. You can also use the extra quinoa to stir into casseroles or sauces once they are cooked to bulk them out and for added nutritional value. To make quinoa ratatouille, lightly fry **1 chopped onion** and **2 crushed garlic cloves** in **2 tablespoons olive oil**. Add **1 diced red bell pepper** and **1 diced yellow or orange bell pepper, 2 diced zucchini** and **½ diced eggplant**. Cook a couple of minutes, then add **1 can (15-oz.) crushed tomatoes, 2 tablespoons ketchup**, ½ **teaspoon Italian herbs** and season with a little **sea salt** and **freshly ground black pepper**. Cover with a lid and simmer 30 minutes. Makes 2 adult and 2 child portions.

We are in adult territory now so don't let the kids get their hands on any leftovers! If you like, replace the sloe gin with Southern Comfort, and for more variety use blackberry-, lemon-, orange- or strawberry-flavored gelatin. You can also substitute orange segments, strawberries or sliced peaches for the summer berries.

Sloe Gin Jellies with Minted Crème Fraîche

MAKES 4 adult portions
PREPARATION TIME 5 minutes, plus cooling and at least 4 hours setting

FOR THE SLOE GIN JELLIES
1¼ cups apple juice
2 envelopes (¼-oz.) raspberry-flavored gelatin
¾ cup plus 2 tablespoons sloe gin
1⅔ cups mixed summer berries (blueberries, raspberries, strawberries and blackberries)

FOR THE MINTED CRÈME FRAÎCHE
1 handful mint leaves, finely chopped, plus extra leaves to decorate
¾ cup plus 2 tablespoons half-fat crème fraîche or sour cream
½ lemon
2 tablespoons confectioners' sugar, sifted

1 Put the apple juice in a measuring jug or bowl with the gelatin and microwave on High 1 minute. Remove and stir until the gelatin dissolves. Stir in the sloe gin. Leave to cool.

2 Divide the berries among 4 glasses or small bowls, then pour the cooled gelatin over the tops. Put in the refrigerator to set for at least 4 hours.

3 To make the minted crème fraîche, stir the mint into the crème fraîche with a squeeze of lemon juice and the confectioners' sugar. (The gelatins and crème fraîche can be prepared a day in advance, covered with plastic wrap and kept in the refrigerator.)

4 Remove the gelatins from the refrigerator, decorate with mint leaves and serve with the minted crème fraîche spooned on top or handed around separately.

My other name for this is the Easiest Pudding You Can Wish For. Serve this on its own or with cookies or shortbread. It's also nice with a mixed berry salad: chopped strawberries, blueberries, raspberries and blackberries tossed in a little confectioners' sugar. If you prefer, you can simply leave out the rosemary, or, for a bit of variety, use half lemon and half lime juice. A finely chopped piece of preserved ginger and 2 tablespoons ginger syrup from the jar spice it up wonderfully, while the seeds of 6 cardamom pods infused with the milk and then strained, give the basic recipe another new set of flavors.

Lemon and Rosemary Posset

MAKES 4 individual possets
PREPARATION TIME 10 minutes, plus cooling and at least 2 hours chilling
COOKING TIME 4 minutes

2 rosemary sprigs
2 cups plus 2 tablespoons heavy cream
¾ cup sugar
⅓ cup lemon juice

1 Bruise the rosemary by hitting lightly with a rolling pin (the kids will think you are mad if they see you doing this!) and put in a saucepan with the cream and sugar. Gently bring to a boil, stirring to dissolve the sugar. Reduce the heat to low and simmer 3 minutes, stirring occasionally and making sure the cream doesn't boil.

2 Remove the pan from the heat, fish out the rosemary and leave the cream to cool a few minutes before stirring in the lemon juice.

3 Pour into wine glasses, dishes or cups and leave to cool, then put in the refrigerator at least 2 hours to chill. (The lemon posset can be made a couple of days before serving and kept covered in the refrigerator.)

Everyone loves a chocolate dessert to round off a delicious meal, so imagine the "oooohs" you'll get serving three mini ones to everyone. These recipes are simple to put together (two can be made in advance), look great all together on one plate and taste fantastic.

Triple Chocolate Dessert

EACH ONE MAKES 4 adult portions
PREPARATION TIME 10 minutes each, plus chilling

SUPER EASY CHOCOLATE MOUSSE

3½ ounces dark chocolate, 70% cocoa solids, broken into pieces
7 tablespoons heavy cream
½ cup bought or Foolproof Homemade Custard Sauce (see page 114)
4 tablespoons your favorite liqueur (optional)

1 Put the chocolate in a large, heatproof bowl. Rest the bowl over a pan of simmering water so the bottom of the bowl does not touch the water. Stir occasionally until the chocolate melts.

2 Whisk the cream until it just forms soft peaks, then fold in the custard sauce, liqueur, if using, and melted chocolate. Spoon into four espresso cups or little glasses and chill at least 30 minutes.

BLACK FOREST CREAM CRUNCH

2 tablespoons cherry jam
7 tablespoons heavy cream, lightly whipped
1 tablespoon kirsch liqueur or cherry brandy (optional)
⅔ cup fresh cherries, pitted, or canned or macerated cherries
4 chocolate cookies, chocolate-coated graham crackers or crunchy cookies, crushed to a crumb
1 tablespoon grated dark chocolate, 70% cocoa solids

1 Mix together the cherry jam, whipped cream and kirsch, if using.

2 Layer the mixture with the cherries and cookie crumbs in four small glasses. Chill until needed.

3 When ready to serve, sprinkle with grated chocolate.

BOOZY ICED BERRIES AND HOT WHITE CHOCOLATE SAUCE

9 ounces mixed frozen berries, thawed and drained
⅓ cup heavy cream
2¾ ounces white chocolate, broken into small pieces
4 tablespoons crème de cassis

1 Divide the berries into four small glasses or little plates. Leave them in the refrigerator about 20 minutes before serving.

2 Just before serving, gently melt the cream and chocolate together in a small saucepan over a low heat or in the microwave.

3 Pour the cassis over the berries, then pour the white chocolate sauce over just as you serve them.

The subtle coconut and orange flavor of these rich, creamy Italian desserts is perfectly balanced by the tangy, juicy rhubarb, and this rounds any meal off with style. I like to leave the panna cottas to set in glasses, which saves the hassle of turning them out of molds when serving, but you can leave then to set in lightly greased 7-ounce teacups, gelatin molds, ramekins or dariole molds, if you prefer.

Coconut and Orange Panna Cotta with Rhubarb Compote

MAKES 4 adult portions
PREPARATION TIME 20 minutes, plus at least 3 hours setting (overnight if possible)
COOKING TIME 35 minutes

FOR THE PANNA COTTA
a little vegetable oil, for greasing
2 teaspoons unflavored powdered gelatin or 4 leaves gelatin
1½ cups plus 2 tablespoons coconut milk
¾ cup plus 2 tablespoons heavy cream
peeled zest of 1 orange
scant 1 cup confectioners' sugar
⅔ cup plain yogurt

FOR THE RHUBARB COMPOTE
1⅔ cups rhubarb cut into 1-inch pieces
¼ cup sugar
2 tablespoons orange juice

1 Put the powdered gelatin in a small dish, sprinkle 3 tablespoons water over and leave 5 minutes, or until the water is absorbed. Alternatively, if you are using gelatin leaves, soak them in cold water 5 minutes, or until soft.

2 Put the coconut milk, cream and orange zest in a saucepan over medium heat and stir in the confectioners' sugar. Gently bring to a boil, stirring occasionally. If you are using leaf gelatin, squeeze out the excess water. Remove the pan from the heat and stir in the soaked or squeezed gelatin until it dissolves. Leave to cool 5 minutes.

3 Stir in the yogurt until smooth, using a whisk, if necessary. Strain through a strainer into a large measuring jug, then pour into the glasses, leave to cool completely and chill in the refrigerator at least 3 hours, or overnight, if you can.

4 Heat the oven to 275°F.

5 To prepare the rhubarb compote, mix together the rhubarb, sugar and orange juice and put in a roasting pan, arranging the rhubarb in a flat layer. Bake the rhubarb 30 minutes until it is tender and the juice is syrupy. Leave to cool. (The panna cottas and the rhubarb can be made a day in advance and kept in the refrigerator.)

6 Spoon some rhubarb compote on top of the panna cottas with a little of the syrup to serve.

Chocolate and caramel are a match made in heaven, but add a little sea salt to the mixture and it takes the flavors to another level. I really urge you to try this recipe—there are no excuses, because it can easily be made the day before you need it. (If you really are struggling for time, check out the How to make, below.) This makes a large tart so there's plenty for four adults, plus leftovers for the kids.

Chocolate and Salted Caramel Tart

MAKES a 9-inch tart
PREPARATION TIME 20 minutes,
   plus cooling
COOKING TIME 20 minutes

FOR THE TART
5½ ounces dark chocolate, 70% cocoa
   solids, broken into small pieces
4 eggs, lightly beaten
½ cup superfine sugar
5 tablespoons butter, melted
½ cup less 1 tablespoon all-purpose
   flour, sifted
9-inch bought sweet pastry case

FOR THE SALTED CARAMEL SAUCE
½ cup soft light brown sugar
5 tablespoons butter
2½ tablespoons golden syrup or light
   corn syrup
½ cup double cream
1 teaspoon flaked sea salt, plus extra
   to taste

TO SERVE
confectioners' sugar, for dusting
vanilla ice cream
dark and white chocolate

1 Heat the oven to 350°F.

2 To make the chocolate tart, put the chocolate in a large heatproof bowl. Rest the bowl over a pan of gently simmering water so the bottom of the bowl does not touch the water. Stir occasionally until the chocolate melts. (Alternatively, melt the chocolate gently in the microwave.) Beat in the eggs, sugar, butter and flour.

3 Put the pastry case on a cookie sheet, and pour in the chocolate filling. Transfer to the oven and bake 15 minutes, or until just set. Remove and leave to cool to room temperature on a wire rack. (The tart can be made a day ahead and left at room temperature for a softer filling.)

4 To make the sauce, put the brown sugar, butter and golden syrup in a saucepan over low heat and stir until the butter melts. Bring to a simmer about 3 minutes, swirling the pan a couple of times. Add the cream and salt and cook a minute longer. Taste (it will be super hot) and add more salt, if you like. Transfer to a measuring jug and leave to cool. (This can be made a few days ahead and kept in the refrigerator.)

5 When ready to serve, warm the sauce to a spoonable consistency and drizzle over slices of the tart. Using a vegetable peeler, slowly shave over pieces of the dark and white chocolate, creating little curls, then dust with confectioners' sugar and add a scroll of ice cream on the confectioners' sugar. (The sugar stops the ice cream from sliding around.)

How to make
cheat's chocolate and salted caramel tart

If time really isn't on your side, there is nothing wrong with embelishing bought products to create an impressive dessert. If you don't want to give the game away, just hide the packaging! Buy a simple **chocolate tart** or **torte** and cut into generous slices. Gently heat **1 tablespoon bought dulce de leche** or **caramel sauce** per person in the microwave until it reaches a spoonable consistency, then stir in **¼ teaspoon flaked sea salt** per person. Serve as above, and let your guests praise you for your creativity.

I love making brownies and adding exciting flavors to them. Chocolate and ginger is a wonderful, classic combination and the preserved ginger makes the finished result sticky, chewy and amazing! This recipe makes a generous quantity so there's plenty for you to enjoy over a few days. Just store the brownies in an airtight container.

Chocolate and Ginger Brownies with Ginger Cream

MAKES 12 squares
PREPARATION TIME 20 minutes,
  plus cooling
COOKING TIME 25 minutes

FOR THE BROWNIES
1 cup less 2 tablespoons butter (1¾ sticks), plus extra for greasing
7 ounces dark chocolate, 70% cocoa solids, broken into small pieces
6 tablespoons finely chopped preserved ginger
1 teaspoon sea salt
3 eggs
1½ cups sugar
1 teaspoon vanilla extract
1 cup all-purpose flour
1 tablespoon unsweetened cocoa powder

FOR THE GINGER CREAM
¾ cup plus 2 tablespoons heavy or whipping cream
3 tablespoons preserved ginger syrup

1 Heat the oven to 350°F. Grease a deep 8- x 12-inch baking pan and line with parchment paper.

2 Put the butter and chocolate in a large heatproof bowl. Rest the bowl over a pan of gently simmering water so the bottom of the bowl does not touch the water. Stir occasionally until the chocolate melts. (Alternatively, melt the chocolate gently in a microwave.) Stir in the ginger and salt.

3 Using an electric mixer, beat together the eggs, sugar and vanilla extract until they are thick and creamy. Mix in the melted chocolate. Finally, sift the flour over and stir to combine. Pour into the prepared baking pan. Place in the oven and bake 25 minutes, or until the top is cracking and the middle is just set. It might seem too soon to remove the baking pan from the oven, but the batter will continue to bake after after the pan is out of the oven. As soon as you remove the pan from the oven, dust the top of the brownie mixture with the cocoa powder.

4 Leave the brownies to cool in the baking pan about 20 minutes before turning out and cutting into squares to save for later. (The brownies can be made several hours before you need them—but keep them in a secret place so the kids can't get them.)

5 To make the cream, whisk together the cream and ginger syrup until it forms soft peaks.

6 Serve the brownies warm or cold with the ginger cream.

This is a stunning dessert, but the pavlova loses its impact if it's only small so I always make a large one. The guests appreciate it and we get lots left to enjoy the next day! As a treat for the kids, keep back some of the meringue and spoon small dollops (the size of a small walnut) onto a baking sheet. Put into the oven with the pavlova for just an hour. When they are cool, sandwich them together in pairs with a little whipped cream and jam or a chocolate spread to make what my children call "meringue kisses".

Limoncello and Blackberry Pavlova

MAKES 6 to 8 adult portions
PREPARATION TIME 20 minutes, plus cooling
COOKING TIME 1½ hours

4 egg whites
1 cup superfine sugar
2 teaspoons cornstarch
2 teaspoons lemon juice
1 cup plus 2 tablespoon heavy cream
4 tablespoons limoncello liqueur
2⅓ cups blackberries
grated lemon zest, to decorate

1 Heat the oven to 275°F and line a cookie sheet with parchment paper.

2 Using an electric mixer, whisk the egg whites in a large bowl until stiff peaks form. Mix together the sugar and cornstarch, then whisk that mixture into the egg whites, a spoonful at a time, adding the lemon juice with the last spoonful. Continue to whisk a minute or so until the meringue is thick and glossy.

3 Spoon onto the prepared cookie sheet and spread to form a circle about 8½ inch diameter, leaving a dip in the middle for the cream filling. Bake about 1½ hours until the meringue is crisp. Remove from the oven and leave to cool on the cookie sheet. (The meringue can be made 24 hours in advance and stored in an airtight container.)

4 To finish the pavlova, whisk the cream with the limoncello until it forms soft peaks. Reserve half of the blackberries for decoration, then lightly crush the rest with the back of a spoon. Fold the crushed berries into the cream and spoon the mixture into the middle of the pavlova. Top with the remaining berries, then sprinkle with grated lemon zest. Serve within an hour of adding the cream.

How to make
chocolate pavlova
Simply add ¼ **cup sifted unsweetened cocoa powder** with the sugar. For extra chocolatey loveliness, stir in **5 ounces milk chocolate chips** or **broken chocolate buttons**. Use plain whipped cream and mix in **raspberries**, **strawberries** or **canned cherries**. Decorate with **grated chocolate**.

Cook these on the barbecue or use a griddle on the stovetop to make a light and refreshing end to a meal. Raspberries or a mixture of summer fruits can be used in place of strawberries. I suggest you use Pimm's if you can find it, but Southern Comfort works just as well.

Griddled Peaches with Strawberry Cream

MAKES 4 adult portions
PREPARATION TIME 15 minutes, plus
  2 hours marinating
COOKING TIME 2 minutes

⅓ cup Southern Comfort or Pimm's
  No.1 Cup
3 tablespoons confectioners' sugar, plus
  extra for dusting
1 vanilla bean, halved with seeds
  removed
4 ripe peaches, halved and pitted
¾ cup plus 2 tablespoon heavy cream
1⅓ cups strawberries, stems removed
  and halved or quartered if large

1 Mix together the Southern Comfort, confectioners' sugar and vanilla seeds. Put the peach halves in a shallow bowl, pour the Southern Comfort mixture over and cover with plastic wrap. Macerate the peaches in the refrigerator a couple hours, or overnight, if you can.

2 When you're ready to cook, put a griddle over high heat or have your barbecue super hot. Lift the peaches out of the marinade and dust the cut surfaces with confectioners' sugar. Put the peaches sugar-side down on the griddle or barbecue and broil 1 minute, or until the sugar caramelizes.

3 Put 3 tablespoons of the marinade in a bowl and the rest in a small saucepan. Boil the marinade in the pan 1 minute until it becomes syrupy.

4 Meanwhile, whisk the cream with the reserved marinade until it just starts to form soft peaks.

5 Spoon the syrup over the peaches. Fold the strawberries through the cream and serve with the griddled peaches.

Leftovers for chocolate indulgence
vanilla hot chocolate

I also like to treat myself to this indulgent hot chocolate when I get a moment to relax. To make 1 adult- or 2 kid-size cups, put **1 cup plus 2 tablespoons milk** in a saucepan with the **split and scraped vanilla bean**. Very slowly bring to a simmer, stirring occasionally: the longer it takes, the more vanilla flavor will infuse into the milk. Remove the pan from the heat and stir in **1¾ ounces chopped dark chocolate, 70% cocoa solids**, until it melts. Remove the vanilla bean and pour the chocolate milk into your favorite cup. Serve as it is or, for a bigger treat, top with **marshmallows** and **whipped cream**.

Many recipes tell you to put the leftover vanilla bean in a jar of sugar to flavor it for baking. I like to keep one in a covered container of fresh eggs. If you keep them in the refrigerator, they take on a subtle vanilla flavor through the porous shells, making them great for baking and sweet recipes.

Try this light, yet rich, flourless cake if you have to cater for someone who doesn't eat gluten, although you don't have to save it for them, because the whole family will love it. This recipe makes a large cake so there's plenty for leftovers to enjoy through the week.

Chocolate, Coconut and Raspberry Torte

MAKES 8 adult portions
PREPARATION TIME 15 minutes
COOKING TIME 40 minutes

¾ cup butter, plus extra for greasing
6 ounces dark chocolate, 70% cocoa
    solids, broken into small pieces
¾ cup sugar
6 eggs, separated
1¾ cups shredded coconut, plus extra
    for sprinkling
1 cup raspberries
confectioners' sugar, for dusting

1 Heat the oven to 350°F. Grease a 9-inch cake pan with butter and line the bottom with parchment paper.

2 Put the chocolate in a large, heatproof bowl. Rest the bowl over a pan of simmering water so the bottom of the bowl does not touch the water. Stir occasionally until the chocolate melts. (Alternatively, melt the chocolate gently in a microwave.)

3 Using an electric mixer, beat the butter and sugar until light and creamy. Thoroughly beat in one egg yolk at a time, then add the melted chocolate and shredded coconut, mixing until combined.

4 Using the electric mixer with clean beaters, in a clean bowl, beat the egg whites until semi-stiff peaks form. Stir one-third of the egg whites into the chocolate mixture to lighten the batter, then gently fold in the remaining egg whites using a large metal spoon. Spoon into the prepared cake pan. Put in the oven and bake 35 to 40 minutes until a skewer inserted into the middle comes out clean.

5 Leave to cool in the pan about 10 minutes, then transfer to a serving plate. When ready to serve, pile the raspberries on top and dust with confectioners' sugar mixed with a little coconut.

Leftovers for the kids
chocolate cake pops

If you have any torte left over, the kids will love you for ever if you make these. Break the **leftover torte** into fine crumbs and mix in just enough **raspberry jam** to bind together. Shape into truffle-size balls and put in the freezer 15 minutes to chill. Dip the tip of lollipop sticks into a small bowl of **melted chocolate** (dark, semisweet, milk or white) and insert it into the middle of the chilled balls. Then dip each cake pop into the melted chocolate to cover evenly. Tap the stick to drip excess chocolate back into the bowl, then push the stick into something like a piece of polystyrene or even a large potato with a flat base (this brings back memories of cheese and pineapple on sticks). When the chocolate is almost, but not quite, set, scatter sprinkles over and leave to set completely.

Index